TROUT AND TERRESTRIALS

TROUT AND TERRESTRIALS

Lou Stevens

SWAN·HILL
PRESS

I have fond memories of many worthwhile adversaries who have obliged by
taking my terrestrial offerings.
Without those gallant trout this book would never have been written.

Copyright © 1993 by Lou Stevens

First published in the UK in 1993
by Swan Hill Press an imprint of Airlife Publishing Ltd

British Library Cataloguing in Publication Data
A catalogue record for this book is available
from the British Library

ISBN 1 85310 388 8

Printed by Livesey Ltd, Shrewsbury

Swan Hill Press
an imprint of Airlife Publishing Ltd.
101 Longden Road, Shrewsbury SY3 9EB.

Acknowledgements

I wish to thank my good friend, fellow flyfisher and entomologist, Edward J. Blane PhD, for his patient work identifying a number of my more obscure specimen insects.

Thanks are also due to my brother, Gerry Stevens, who willingly offered his studio facilities to photograph my many fly patterns.

Last but not least, I must mention Ed Bassin, Roy Stoddard and Martin Kelner QC, good friends and fishing companions, who were always ready to accept my patterns and report their results.

Contents

List of Figures

Foreword

Many years ago, more years than I care to remember, I received a fly-fishing outfit for my eighth birthday. Up to that age my fishing had been restricted to roach in the local pond, with maggots dangling below a huge red-topped float.

My progress as a fly-fisherman was limited by lack of funds, and a home situated a very long way from any trout water. However, I did progress, serving a hard apprenticeship fly-fishing for coarse fish.

After military service, and a relocation to live and work in Canada, I managed to 'graduate' to trout. Unlimited trout!

Over the years, trout fishing became more than a pastime, it became an obsession.

One day, idly looking through some research papers from the University of British Columbia, I was surprised to learn that, during the summer months, 65 per cent of a trout's diet consisted of terrestrial insects.

What a revelation! Now the 'dog days' of high summer were explained. Now I realised why standard flies brought such poor results on those magnificent days of late June, July and August.

Once I was started on the terrestrial road, there was no turning back. No longer was I an early and late-season fisher; now only the limitations of my own ingenuity prevented my taking trout the whole season through.

The years that have passed, and the myriad of patterns tied and tested, have proved beyond all question that to ignore terrestrial fishing is to forfeit a third of the season's best fishing.

Through this book I would like to share my experience and to pass on to other fly-fishers the result of those years of work and experimentation. The failures have been many – but the successes have more than made up for them.

Add terrestrials to your fly-box and enjoy good fishing throughout the season. There are so many fine trout waiting to be caught!

Lou Stevens
Alvaston

CHAPTER 1

The Food of Trout

During the summer months the daily preoccupation of trout is the quest for food. True, this is necessarily governed by the requirements of safety, but food in its various forms must be found on an almost continuous basis.

The food of trout is more varied than most anglers realise. Almost any insect or small creature that comes within the trout's field of vision is considered, some are rejected because for various reasons they are known to be unpalatable, or the trout is satiated with food at that moment. However, almost all items of possible food are carefully appraised.

Common items of food are winged insects, both water-bred and terrestrial, nymphal forms of flies, terrestrial insects that find themselves in or on the water, worms, small crustaceans, the colony of small aquatic insects and on occasion fish fry.

The months of high summer, when terrestrial insects are most abundant and active, happens to coincide with the period when water-bred fly hatches are sparse during the day. Trout are back in good condition and require a regular intake of food, but at the same time are inclined to be inactive during bright, hot, sunny days, preferring to seek shady lies and to restrict their feeding to early morning and evening. Do not misunderstand this situation: the trout has not lost interest in food; it is simply that hatching flies are not available in sufficient quantity to warrant the expenditure of energy required to take up a feeding station. Also, the bright conditions of open water spell danger from predators which are extremely active at such times. But if food that can be taken with a minimum of effort confronts the trout, and safety conditions are acceptable, then the interest is still there.

All water is bounded by land, and terrestrial insects very often find themselves in or on the water through circumstances beyond their control. Grasshoppers and crickets jump in any direction and often alight on nearby water, and flying insects are blown by the wind. Many terrestrial flying insects mate on the wing and are liable to fall 'spent' to the water surface. Caterpillars and leafhoppers fall from overhanging foliage. Numerous non-flying terrestrial insects are washed into the water during periods of rain. Many terrestrial moths and midges are attracted by the reflection of the water surface. Such mishaps are common, and all present the trout with the opportunity of food at the expenditure of little energy, often within the confines of their safe lie.

The fly-fisherman, aware of these circumstances, is able to convert the unpromising hot days of high summer to a productive period. Instead of confining his activities to early morning or evening hatches, or idly prospecting with a non-productive dry fly, he is able to fish likely lies with a terrestrial imitation, very often with spectacular results.

Although fishing a terrestrial imitation makes a lot of sense, full rewards will never be achieved by just having a few so-called terrestrial patterns in a corner of the fly-box. No serious fly-fisher would consider it reasonable to tie an unknown nondescript fly to his tippet and then cast it willy-nilly in the hope of catching a fish. However, this is very often the attitude adopted where terrestrial patterns are concerned.

The professional fly-tying houses are partly to blame for this apathetic approach. Too often their lists contain such items as 'Beetle', 'Ant', 'Caterpillar', 'Moth' etc, etc: no particular insect is imitated and the inference is that a general pattern will suffice. Experienced anglers who would be aghast if standard fly patterns were treated in the same manner are often prepared to accept such non-specific terrestrial patterns.

Adopting such a cavalier attitude towards a major part of the trout's diet will not bring the desired results. True, the odd fish will be taken, but consistent satisfying results will remain elusive, and the fly-fisher will soon discard terrestrial patterns in favour of standard flies.

The above comments show that more study is necessary if the potential of terrestrials is to be fully realised. It is the intention, in the following pages, to consider the terrestrial insects that lend themselves to such exploitation, and at the same time the fly-tying techniques that will enable us to imitate them.

In the past, very little work has been done in this direction. True, many terrestrial patterns have emerged, but compared to the amount of work that has taken place to evolve standard wet and dry flies, nymphs, etc, the commitment has been minimal. What a pity! Terrestrials form such a large part of the trout's daily diet during midsummer that they are of paramount importance if good fishing is to be enjoyed throughout the season.

A book of this nature cannot hope to cover all terrestrial insects that may find themselves on or in the water. Insect life also varies from region to region, but it is hoped to discuss the common species so as to introduce the angler to fishing the terrestrial imitation. From this simple beginning more work must follow, further patterns must evolve, so that in time all flyboxes will contain a selection of these very important imitations.

CHAPTER 2

Beetles

Most, but not all, beetles encountered in the UK belong to the order *Coleoptera*, which is a very large order divided into many sub-orders and families. In fact, well over 3,000 insects in the UK are classified as *Coleoptera*.

From an angling standpoint a study of such a large order has little relevance, but a study of common beetles is indeed necessary. Many beetles accidentally find themselves in or on the water, and most varieties are avidly taken by trout.

It would be a frustrating exercise to attempt to classify every beetle seen near water. It would also be somewhat futile, as beetles are mostly in or on the water on a 'one-off' basis. However, this is not always the case; many instances occur when a particular beetle is prolific in the area, or large numbers of a certain beetle suddenly become very active. A lot depends on the time of the year, with weather conditions sometimes having an important bearing on what is taking place.

Many beetles are generally common, while some that are local to certain areas may be totally absent from another. It is not intended to exclude beetles from our discussion simply because they are regional in distribution. The important point is whether or not they lend themselves to imitation. When a beetle is presented to the trout on a 'one-off' basis it matters very little whether it is local or not. Beetles are extremely difficult to imitate at the best of times, and if we are to present to the trout a worthwhile pattern that will deceive, then we must be selective as to which beetles we imitate.

When there is a virtual plague of a particular insect locally it would obviously pay dividends to simulate the species. The writer often fishes a favourite river in Wales that winds its way through a heavily wooded valley. Almost always, for a short period each summer, the woods abound with a particular beetle, believed to be a leaf beetle of the *Donacia* species. Time spent evolving an appropriate imitation has paid very handsome dividends.

Many beetles fly in bright sunlight and, by mishap, find themselves on the water by day. Others are confirmed nocturnal flyers, and being attracted to light, crash into the reflections on the water surface. Most beetles die quickly when in the water, but are quite buoyant and inclined to float and ride along the current. Very often the hard wing-cases open slightly in death and the tips of wings can be seen protruding beyond the body.

The most common beetles found on water are probably the chafers of the family *Scarabaeidae*. There are more than seventy different chafers in the UK, but most are the same general shape (see Fig. 1). The colours and size vary enormously.

The chafer beetle (*Cetonia cupria*) is a typical example, found mostly in the north of England. The coloration is difficult to describe, though black with an overlay of brilliant metallic green would be close. It is a large beetle, reaching ⅝–⅞ inch in size as an adult. The most active period is from June to August when it can often be seen flying in bright sunshine. Unlike most beetles it can fly without raising the wing-cases and therefore looks considerably smaller in flight than its true size.

A very close relative, the rose chafer (*Cetonia aurata*), occurs mainly in the southern regions of the UK. Its appearance and habits are almost identical to those of the chafer beetle.

Another chafer common to most regions is the garden chafer (*Phyllopertha horticola*). This insect is active by day during June and July and they often swarm in large numbers over grasslands and crops. The garden chafer is not a large beetle ⅜–½ inch in length is average; the head and thorax are black and the wing-cases a metallic red-brown. The underside of this beetle is a greeny colour and quite hairy.

The well-known 'maybug' or cockchafer (*Melolontha melolontha*) is only common in the southern regions of the UK, and consequently many so called 'maybugs' are, in fact, either chafer beetles (*Melolontha hippocastani*) or summer chafers (*Amphimallon solstitialis*). Both are close relatives of the cockchafer and much more widely distributed. The chafer beetle is larger than the summer chafer but an adult length of ¾ inch could be taken as an average for both. These chafers are almost identical in shape, but whereas the chafer beetle has a brown head and thorax with powdery white wing-cases, the summer chafer is all brown and decidedly hairy.

All the 'maybugs' are evening flyers, swarming among the tree-tops in vast numbers during high summer. They are attracted by the water's reflective surface and often crash heavily on to the water. The heavy, splashy rises that are often heard at dusk are not necessarily trout rising to moths or sedges; it could well be 'maybugs' that are being taken.

Ground beetles are also quite common in most localities, and there are many varieties of them with various habits. In general they are the shiny black beetles with narrow heads and ridged wing-cases that are encountered almost everywhere. Several varieties can be quite large, but an average length for imitative purposes would be ⅜–⅝ inch. (see Fig. 1).

The ground beetle (*Feronia caerulescens*) is a typical example of the species. The adults emerge in the spring and are quite active until October. Most of the activity

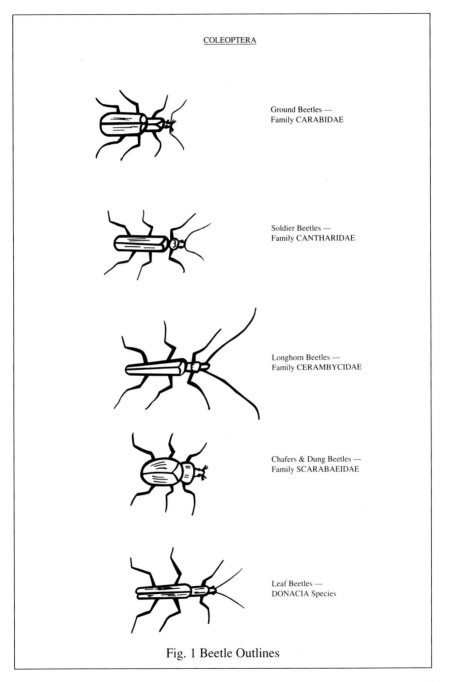

COLEOPTERA

Ground Beetles —
Family CARABIDAE

Soldier Beetles —
Family CANTHARIDAE

Longhorn Beetles —
Family CERAMBYCIDAE

Chafers & Dung Beetles —
Family SCARABAEIDAE

Leaf Beetles —
DONACIA Species

Fig. 1 Beetle Outlines

takes place by day over grasslands, but as a result of various mishaps the beetle is very often to be found on the water, offering itself as a food item to a waiting trout.

There is one ground beetle, quite distinctive from the others, that is often encountered in marshy areas. The ground beetle (*Chlaenius nigricornis*) is about ½ inch long and very brightly coloured. The head is copper green in colour, the thorax brown and the wing-cases a greeny yellow. The legs are yellow and black. It is active from May to August. Although it is a pretty beetle, interesting to find and observe, it is hardly worth imitation when other beetles are so numerous.

The dung beetle (*Aphodius rufipes*) is a small beetle, ½–⅝ inch in size, that is active by day and night. At dusk it is attracted to water reflections and is often found on the water surface. It has a keen sense of smell and is attracted to areas where there are a number of cow-pats. If grazing land is adjacent to water, particularly at points where cows drink, then the dung beetle can be expected in goodly numbers between May and August. It is a very rounded, all black, shiny beetle with the head and thorax very wide, and forming, with the wing cases, an almost humped look. There are over forty varieties of dung beetles, but they are all so similar that no differentation need be made.

Soldier beetles are also quite common, there being about sixteen varieties in the UK. They are slow-flying predators, living on various small insects. Very common over woods and meadows where wild flowers are growing, they can often be seen resting immobile on the leaves of flowers waiting for prey to come within range (see Fig. 1).

The soldier beetle (*Cantharis livida*) is typical. It is an elongated beetle with an overall length of ½–⅝ inch as an adult. It is active during May and June. The colour is quite distinctive, an orange head and thorax with the wing-cases dark grey, edged with browny orange. The same beetle is often found with a different coloration, being all brown, but this is only a regional variation.

Longhorn beetles look very similar to soldier beetles in shape but are easily distinguished by the very long antennae. There are many varieties of these beetles, some sixty in the UK, and they have a wide variety of coloration, some with dark red wing-cases, others with greeny olive wing-cases. Most have a black head, thorax, and antennae (see Fig. 1).

The longhorn beetle (*Strangalia maculata*) is by far the most interesting to imitate. It is active during July and August and is about ½–⅝ inch long. Being a nectar and pollen feeder it is usually found in the vicinity of wild flowers. The shape is similar to that of other longhorns, but the coloration is distinctive. The head and thorax are black, but wing-cases, legs and antennae are yellow and black-striped, wasp-style. They are common in the southern regions of the UK, but tend to become rather rare towards the north.

The remaining beetles that we need to discuss are the leaf beetles. Again there are many varieties, fifteen in all, but nearly all are of the *Donacia* species (see

Fig. 1). They are truly beautiful beetles ⅜–½ inch long. All have an iridescent metallic lustre over the head, thorax and wing-cases – a golden greeny brown. They love the hot bright sunny days and are ready flyers in hot weather. The *Donacia* species are always found in the vicinity of water plants – in fact the larvae are aquatic.

As mentioned previously, the writer has encountered vast numbers of these beetles and had very good results with imitations. The largest wild brown ever taken on a Welsh fishing trip fell to an imitation leaf beetle.

It will now be appreciated that beetles come in a variety of shapes, sizes and colours, but when we discuss the tying of imitations we will be able to reduce the number of patterns required by grouping the varieties.

Fishing the beetle is a fascinating way to take trout. Usually it is a matter of tempting a lethargic fish on a very hot day, or sometimes offering our imitation to a fish that is rising periodically to some unknown food form, especially when no natural aquatic flies are on the water. At other times we may switch to a beetle imitation at dusk when the resounding rises indicate that something other than moths or sedges is being taken.

The time of the day or night and the conditions will demand several different patterns if we seriously intend to take fish. The old-established deer-hair 'beetle' pattern will very often tempt a trout, particularly at dusk when fish are inclined to be less wary, but daytime fishing, in very bright conditions, necessitates a much more discerning approach.

CHAPTER 3

Tying the Beetles

Almost all lists of flies offered for sale include some type of beetle, usually constructed of deer hair. Most books of fly-fishing instruction also mention the use of beetle patterns. In nearly all cases the beetle imitation is recommended as a first-class terrestrial lure – a 'must' for the midsummer fly-fisher.

All this acknowledgement and praise of the beetle imitation is rather surprising when the situation is carefully considered. It is all very well acknowledging that beetles are high on the diet list of trout in summer; it is a totally different matter trying to capture those trout on some of the beetle imitations on offer. The rough deer-hair beetle often brings very disappointing results, even when conditions for its use are near perfect. This is particularly noticeable when natural beetles are on the water. While it is true that the occasional trout may be taken, this should not be confused with the results possible when closer imitation is used. It is one of the exasperating things about trout, that although generally wary and selective in their choice of food, they will sometimes take all manner of objects with absolute abandon.

Fortunately for the trout, and unfortunately for us, such times are rarer than we think.

Trout *do* like beetles, and certainly we are on the right track when we consider the use of a beetle imitation, but for consistent results we must persevere beyond the rough deer-hair patterns.

One beetle pattern that does bring consistent results is the 'Eric's Beetle', and it would be worthwhile to consider the main characteristics of this pattern in detail.

Eric's Beetle

Hook:	10-12
Silk:	Black
Body:	Yellow wool with peacock herl wound over leaving a yellow butt exposed
Hackle:	Black

When asking ourselves why the Eric's Beetle consistently takes trout it would be as well to remember that it is basically a 'wet' pattern, representing a drowned dead beetle. The peacock herl obviously simulates the fat body outline required and at the same time offers a degree of iridescence often found on beetle wing-cases. The yellow butt gives the impression of an underbody exposed by the wing-cases being slightly opened after death. The hackle probably represents the legs. A simple pattern, yes, but one that covers all the salient points.

Although the Eric's Beetle is a successful pattern, it would be foolish to think it is the only pattern required. After all, we would not contemplate fishing throughout the season using just a single dun pattern. However, the pattern does illustrate that thought given to close representation pays dividends.

The general points to be remembered when tying beetles are:

1. the general outline
2. size
3. the colour
4. the legs and
5. the nature of the wing-cases

Points 1 and 2 do not need any explanation, but items 3, 4, and 5 require considerable thought.

The legs of beetles are totally unlike those of aquatic flies and cannot be adequately represented by a hackle, or a 'fuzz' of deer-hair ends. The legs are substantial and obviously are one of its recognition points to the trout. The number of legs is unimportant – six or eight may be used. It has been found that pheasant-tail fibres tied in as shown in Fig. 3, then trimmed for length, make for a very realistic pattern. For the purist the fibre can be knotted once in the centre of each leg, but this is totally unnecessary – straight legs are perfectly adequate.

The backs of beetle patterns (the wing-cases) require most careful consideration and must be varied according to the beetle being imitated. Beetles vary considerably in colour, and while nearly all may be classed as 'hard-backed', some are quite hairy. The colour may be anything from a dull black to a bright iridescent red or green – or a combination of colours depending on the light. Fig. 2 lists the materials that lend themselves to imitating the wing-cases of various naturals.

Fig. 3 illustrates the general method of tying a beetle pattern and, if the beetle outlines shown in Fig. 1 are followed, the finished lure should give a reasonable impression of the natural. Patterns are shown in Figs. 4 and 5.

A few tips on the tying illustrated in Fig. 3 may be helpful. The underbody material is tied in first (A). The wing-case material is tied in over it and left to extend beyond the hook bend (B). The underbody is then formed as shown in C. The legs are placed in position and held by figure-of-eight tyings of the silk (D);

a drop of varnish or vycoat will secure them in position. The wing-case material is then brought back *tightly* towards the eye of the hook and secured on the hook shank (E). At this stage sufficient space must be left behind the hook eye for a thorax and head to be formed. The finished lure will be as shown in F, with the legs pressed downwards by the wing-case material.

Early patterns were finished off by repeated coats of varnish to the wing-cases. As time passed this proved to be a mistake. If the pattern is ever to be used as a successful floating lure it is essential for fly floatant to penetrate the wing-case material, right down into the underbody. The varnishing was originally intended to represent the shiny hard backs of these insects, but careful choice of material will give exactly the same effect.

Another early innovation was the tying in of hackle points beyond the bend of the hook to represent wings extended beyond the wing-cases after death. A nice touch, but one that did little to enhance the lure or attract trout. Whether such extended wings are tied in or not is a matter of personal choice.

When small beetles are tied with trailing wings they closely resemble emerger dun patterns, and there is a school of thought that they may, therefore, represent more than one variety of food to the trout and be more attractive as a result. Experience has not borne out this theory. It has long been suspected that emerger patterns are mainly effective during an actual hatch of duns, a situation that rarely exists when a beetle imitation is used.

Whenever these lures are used 'dry' it is impossible to control whether or not they land on the water the right way up. The weight of the hook point should, in theory, ensure that they land the correct way up, but very often the 'hump' of the back counteracts the weight of the hook point. Never mind, not all naturals land the same way on water, and the underbody will still ensure that we present a good 'picture' to the trout.

Ground & Dung Beetles

Natural black hair
Synthetic black hair
Black floss

Soldier Beetles & Longhorns

Coloured natural hair
Coloured synthetic hair
Black floss
Natural black hair
Synthetic black hair

Chafer Beetles

Coloured brown hair
'Dirty' white hair
Green peacock herl
Bronze peacock herl

Donacia Species

Peacock herl from the eye
feather of the peacock

Fig. 2 Materials for Beetle Wing-cases

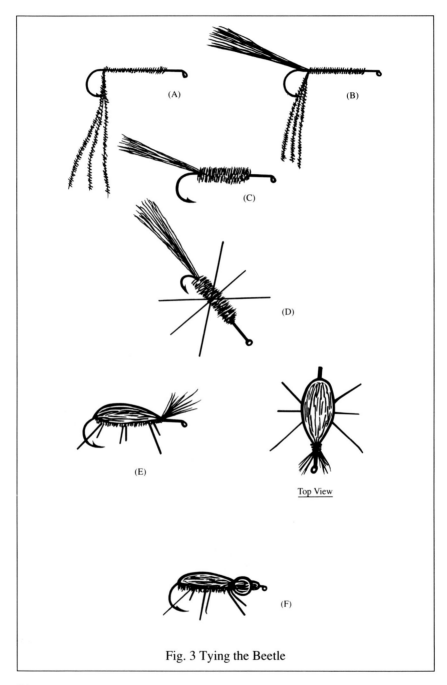

Fig. 3 Tying the Beetle

GROUND BEETLE

Hook   : 12 Long Shank
Wing-cases : Black Hair
Under-body : Black Ostrich herl
Legs   : Pheasant tail fibres
Thorax   : Tying silk
Head   : Tying silk
Silk   : Black

SOLDIER BEETLE

Hook   : 14 Long Shank
Wing-cases : Grey coloured hair
Under-body : Orange Floss
Legs   : Pheasant tail fibres
Thorax   : Tying silk
Head   : Tying silk
Silk   : Orange

LONGHORN BEETLE

Hook   : 14 Long Shank
Wing-cases : Black Hair
Under-body : Black Floss
Legs   : Pheasant tail fibres
Antennae   : Pheasant tail fibres
Thorax   : Tying silk
Head   : Tying silk
Silk   : Black

CHAFER BEETLE

Hook   : 12 Long Shank
Wing-cases : Brown hair, or green,
               or bronze peacock herl
Under-body : Black Ostrich herl
Legs   : Pheasant tail fibres
Thorax   : Tying silk
Head   : Tying silk
Silk   : Black

Fig. 4 Beetle Tying Patterns

<u>DONACIA SPECIES</u>

Hook   : 14 Long Shank
Wing-cases : Bronze Peacock herl
Under-body : Green Floss
Legs   : Pheasant tail fibres
Thorax   : Bronze Peacock herl
Head   : Tying silk
Silk   : Olive

Fig. 5 Beetle Tying Patterns

CHAPTER 4

The Hopper Family

To the large trout the hopper family of insects must represent the ultimate succulent delicacy of high summer. Unfortunately, for the fly-fisherman it is probably the most frustrating terrestrial to imitate and present.

Hoppers are extremely common on grasslands and foliage adjacent to waterways, and although difficult to locate and observe in their natural habitat are really quite active. In the main they hatch during early summer, and as the summer progresses and they become adults their activity increases. Because the hopper has no idea as to where it jumps – it simply jumps in the direction it is facing – it is quite likely to land on water if there is water nearby.

As a terrestrial lure the hopper imitation should rate very highly, but the difficulties are many. The main problem is the size. Most adult hoppers encountered in the UK are ½ – 1¼ inch in length, so imitative lures have to be quite long and very bulky. Casting such a lure is far from easy. Also, it must be appreciated that such a succulent morsel is the prerogative of quite a large trout and well beyond the capacity of the average fish to be found.

Of course, during early summer young hoppers are abundant and, being smaller, they are accessible to smaller trout. But young hoppers are not nearly as active as adults, do not jump the same distances and therefore do not land on water as frequently. The use of a young hopper imitation during early summer is also largely unnecessary as fly hatches occur during the day and fish may be more easily taken by conventional means.

The next difficulty encountered by the fly-fisherman lies in the antics of a hopper when it finds itself on the water. Adult hoppers cause quite a commotion, moving their legs frantically in a rowing action, which, although ineffective, does create considerable movement. Young hoppers are much quieter on the water and often lie as if lifeless. The activity caused by adult hoppers on the water surface is more noticeable on warm, sunny days and creates less difficulty on colder, windy days when hoppers are often blown off course to the water surface.

To summarise, hopper lures are difficult to fish because of their size and bulk. Activity on the water is hard to simulate, and large fish need to be around to make the presentation worthwhile. However, smaller lures to imitate young hoppers can be productive during early summer, especially on colder, windy days when natural fly hatches might be sparse. Such presentations do not require simulated water surface activity, and the size of the imitation will be substantially reduced. Although only fish of several pounds weight are interested in adult hoppers, an average good-size fish of the water may well be interested in the smaller offering.

The presentation of a hopper imitation should follow the accepted practice of dry-fly fishing, but with variations. It is unnecessary for the imitation to alight delicately on the water surface – in fact, a distinct 'plop' is an advantage. Also, the lure should always be presented very close to the bank, preferably under overhanging foliage. Likely shady lies where the larger fish may be encountered should be sought out. Surface activity cannot be simulated, but a reasonably tight and straight cast will cause a slight drag which may create a 'swinging' motion of the lure: this is highly desirable and attractive to the fish.

There will be no mistaking the rise. Trout take hoppers with a slashing action, and hooking the fish presents no difficulty. Trout will move off their station to take a hopper, often a considerable distance, and the take is invariably quite vicious.

The hopper family of insects in the UK is varied and includes grasshoppers, crickets and leaf hoppers. Some make their home on grassland, meadows or farmland, others stay well above ground in foliage. There are also the marshland types which are just as much at home in the water as on land: in fact, some are strong underwater swimmers.

The common green grasshopper (*Omocestus viridulus*) is active between April and October. As an adult it averages nearly an inch in length, but a ½–⅝-inch lure fished during the early months of summer will imitate the young adult. This hopper is most active during the middle of the day, especially when the weather is warm. Like all hoppers the colours can vary tremendously, but generally speaking the predominant colour is green, with the body often black-banded. The natural habitat is on the ground where there are extensive grasslands.

Often when approaching a grassy bank the angler will disturb several of these green grasshoppers without realising what has occurred. They are not high jumpers and very often just move through the tall grass, not necessarily away from what has disturbed them, for they do not select their direction, but jump in the direction they are facing. If the angler is lucky, and looks out for it, a disturbed green grasshopper may be observed on the water surface almost under his feet. This will give a wonderful opportunity to observe the behaviour and antics referred to above.

The common field grasshopper (*Chorthippus brunneus*) is an even larger hopper, just over an inch in length. It is most active between May and November, particularly on warm, sunny days. Its natural habitat is on the ground, particularly over farmland. The young adult during early summer can be imitated by a ½–⅝-inch lure. The colour is very dull, predominantly brown-grey, but very often there are yellow markings on the body.

Although the field grasshopper is just as common as *Omocestus viridulus*, it is not found on the water as frequently. It tends to stay in the vicinity of cultivated land where there are growing crops, and is rarely found in rough grass except by misjudgement. However, where cultivated fields are adjacent to the water, it may well be the species most often seen by the fish.

The oak bush cricket (*Meconema thalassinum*) is a smaller hopper, hardly ever attaining a length of more than ¾inch. It is active from May to November, but is very nocturnal. The natural habitat is above ground in foliage, particularly oak trees, and on windy days it is often blown to the water surface. A ½-inch lure will imitate this hopper and should always be fished under overhanging foliage. The colour is a very bright green.

Two hoppers that are commonly found near water are of little use to the angler. The large marsh grasshopper (*Stethophyma grossum*) is far too large, averaging nearly 1½ inches in length. It is very distinctive, with a red, black and yellow coloration, and is often on the water near its natural habitat of marshland, but the size alone takes it out of our consideration.

Another drawback of the marsh grasshopper is that it is so local, occurring mostly in the south. Although many anglers may be acquainted with this insect, it would be a mistake to consider it as a useful lure in all localities.

The leaf hopper (*Cicadella viridis*) is another very common hopper that cannot be represented by a hopper lure: The small size, ¼–⅜inch, hardly places it in the category of a hopper for fishing purposes. It is very common in foliage over water and is quite often found on the water surface. It is a very bright green in colour and sometimes an all-green wet fly – fished dry under the overhanging branches – will bring good results on a hot, bright, sultry day.

Generally speaking the hoppers are the most difficult of terrestrials to imitate successfully and are only of real value when quite large fish are expected. However, there is no getting away from the fact that they are much appreciated by the bigger fish, and efforts at imitation can be very rewarding under the right conditions. The experienced angler, prepared to persevere in pursuit of larger fish, may find considerable satisfaction in the use of hopper imitations against those fish not normally taken on a standard dry fly.

CHAPTER 5

Tying the Hoppers

Although the value of hopper imitations has been appreciated for many years, tying such imitations has always given difficulty.

The earliest patterns (from the USA) were little better than large wet flies that had been given an upward curve to the body. Deren's Hopper was an improvement and the accepted hopper pattern for many years, but is was hardly a true hopper imitation and owed its popularity to being an effective wet-fly pattern. Certainly it was very rarely fished to imitate a hopper on the water surface.

Bill Bennett of the American Flyfishers' Club was probably the first to try and evolve a true hopper imitation. It is now nearly fifty years ago that Marinaro and Bennett worked on the problem together and came up with an imitation made entirely from hollow quills. Marinaro reported considerable success with the quill pattern on the limestone streams of Pennsylvania. However, the quill imitation was extremely bulky – tied to imitate the adult hopper – and Marinaro complained of difficulties in trying to make a decent cast. It must also be appreciated that in Marinaro's heyday the trout in the limestone rivers of Pennsylvania were very large – five pounders were quite common – and that the conditions we face in the UK today are totally different.

If we are to be at all successful in presenting a hopper imitation, we must content ourselves with representations of the immature insect, lightly tied in a manner than makes casting feasible.

In accordance with accepted fly-tying practice it is not necessary to attempt to tie an exact model of a hopper. We must try and evolve a representation that displays the prominent features, correct as to size and colour, and one that will give a sufficiently true impression of a hopper that a trout will accept the offering.

For our purposes the common green grasshopper offers the best subject for imitation. The colour is a fairly constant green, although at times it can be decidedly grey in appearance; however, the immature insect is brighter than the adult and in practice green is the only colour we need consider. There is the added advantage that by concentrating on green we are also imitating the colour of the leaf hopper and the oak bush cricket. If we restrict the use of our immature hopper imitation to situations where grasslands come right to the water's edge under overhanging foliage, and make our presentation as close to the bank as possible, we will have the advantage of representing most of the hopper family.

The hopper imitation must be evolved with various important features in mind. A very long shank hook cannot be used to accommodate the elongated body, as this would place the business end of the hook in the wrong position: it is important that the hook is kept central. The prominent back legs do not need to be fully represented, as the upward sweep of the thicker thigh portion is all that is normally seen. A built-up head and large black eye are very important, as are the antennae. Any form of hackle at the head should be avoided, as this would destroy the general outline and should not be needed to float the lure.

If the illustrations in Fig. 6 are carefully followed, tying a lure that incorporates all the main points mentioned above should present little difficulty. The idea of tying a chenille body on to a quill former so that it can become semi-detached may strike the reader as novel, but the basic idea has been accepted fly-tying practice for many years: John Veniard writing in 1970 mentioned the use of quill formers in his writings several times. It is only the use of this technique on a larger scale for the hopper that is new. It is an extremely practical way to tie this lure, and has the advantage of fine floatibility.

Common Green Grasshopper

Hook:	12 or 14 Long Shank
Silk:	Insect Green
Body:	Fine green chenille on a quill base (semi-detached)
Ribbing:	Black silk
Wings:	Two green saddle hackle tips tied in flat over body
Rear Legs:	Two green saddle hackles that have been specially prepared
Antennae:	Two wisps of pheasant tail
Head:	Built up with green silk and with large painted black eye

A few tips may prove helpful. First select a suitable medium-size wing feather and strip off the fibres so that only the centre quill remains, a 2–3-inch section will be fine. Tie in the thinner end of the quill to the hook shank as shown in A. Next strip the end of a length of fine green chenille and tie on to the quill, then tie in a length of black silk as a ribbing (see B). A drop of cement run onto the quill will help secure the chenille. Holding the end of the quill taut, wind the chenille along the quill, then round both quill and hook shank, forming a semi-detached body (C), then wind the ribbing and cut off the extended part of the quill. Two small green hackles are then tied flat over the body to represent the wings (D).

31

Prepare two green saddle hackle feathers as shown in E and F. An easy way is to wet the feathers and draw the fibres down the centre quill until they form a solid mass ready to tie in. The back legs are then positioned and tied as shown in G, the end of the centre quill being cut off after tying is complete.

All that remains is to finish off the lure by building up the head, positioning the antennae and painting a large black eye (H). *Note:* To imitate the common field grasshopper it is only necessary to change the colour from green to light brown.

The construction of this lure allows for quite easy casting without the annoying whistling noise associated with large lures, or the twisting in the air which often occurs with bulky fixed wing flies. It will cock well on the water and is a reasonable floater if well treated with a silicone floatant.

A fine tippet should not be used as this will impair casting. 3x nylon will prove quite satisfactory and is, in fact, necessary, for we are pursuing above average size fish which will slash viciously if they decide to take our offering.

It will help in the presentation of this lure if the last foot of tippet adjacent to the lure is treated to sink while the remaining leader is greased to float. Such preparations are finicky and time-consuming, but they are well worthwhile as they help impart a slight movement to the lure without excessive drag.

Fuller's Earth powder, mixed to a paste with a little glycerine, has proved the best sinkant: it removes all traces of grease from the nylon and if left for a few moments to dry will stay in place for several casts. Be very careful to keep any sinkant well away from the lure itself.

While the oak bush cricket can be well portrayed by a small version of the common green grasshopper, the smaller leaf hopper is in a different category. An average size of ¼–⅜ inch is far more in keeping with normal fly size than with a lure. It has been previously mentioned that a wet-fly pattern of bright green fished 'dry' will bring the best results. Let us now consider the pattern required in more detail.

The Leaf Hopper

Hook:	16 or 18 Long Shank
Silk:	Insect Green
Body:	Green feather fibre, ribbed with a green cock hackle tied palmer, then trimmed above and below
Wings:	Two slips of green feather tied in flat over body
Head:	Tying silk with large painted yellow eye

Fig. 7 shows the construction in detail. After tying in the ribbing hackle, tie in green feather fibres from a large quill feather and wind along the hook shank from bend to eye to form the body (A). Then wind the green cock hackle palmer style from bend to eye (B). Trim the palmer hackle with scissors above and below the

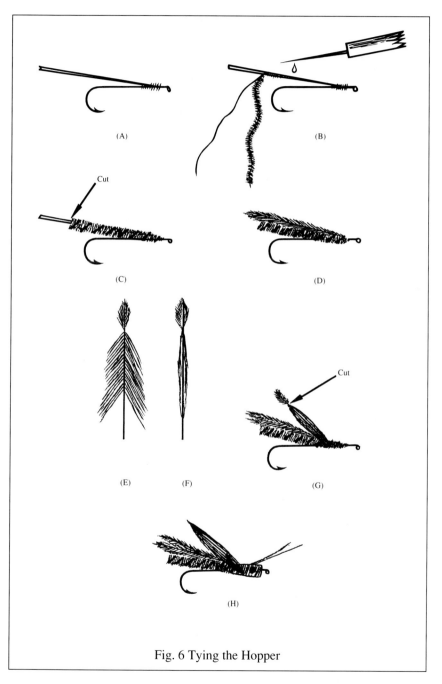

Fig. 6 Tying the Hopper

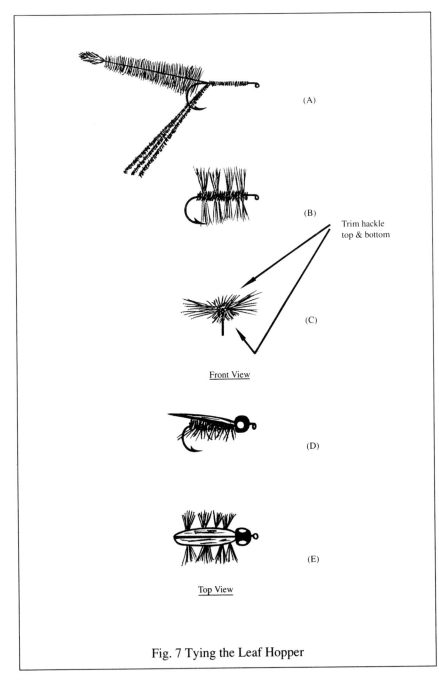

(A)

(B)

Trim hackle
top & bottom

(C)

Front View

(D)

(E)

Top View

Fig. 7 Tying the Leaf Hopper

hook shank so that only the side fibres remain (C), then tie in two slips of green quill feather flat over the body as shown in (D). All that remains is to finish the fly with a prominent head of green silk and paint a yellow eye on either side as in (E).

Flat wings will be more secure and inclined to lie flat if they are raised after tying in and a generous drop of cement is placed on the body of the fly. The wings can then be held down on to the wet, cemented body for a moment until secured.

The leaf hopper imitation does not require any floatant, as the construction is sufficient to ensure a good float. The colour should be the brightest green that the materials available will allow. It must be appreciated that a pattern of this type does not always land on the water the right way up. However, the natural insect, falling from overhanging foliage, does not necessarily fall right way up on the water either, and the construction of the underside of the fly still presents a good illusion to an interested fish.

Fishing the imitation leaf hopper requires exactly the same technique as that used in dry-fly fishing, bearing in mind that the best results will be obtained when fish lies directly under overhanging foliage are explored.

CHAPTER 6

The Wasp Family

It is hard to imagine that the wasp, so detested and avoided by humans, is a luxury titbit to a trout in high summer. Not too many wasps find their way to the water surface, but when they do so they are rarely ignored. Even a trout lying up and almost dormant during the heat of a bright summer's day will suddenly burst into activity at the sight of a wasp trapped in the surface film.

It is not often realised that what is believed to be a 'common wasp' may, in fact, be one of a number of different insects. Even a true wasp may be of several varieties.

Most wasps become active from spring onwards; the fertilised females come out of hibernation and begin to search for nesting sites as the days become warmer. A new nest may be established above or below ground and soon comprises the queen, a number of males and a multitude of workers that are sterile females. It is not uncommon for the population of a wasp nest to exceed 10,000 insects during the high summer months.

An incident comes to mind which took place when the writer was a young lad. I was fishing for roach with several friends when we spotted a wasp nest in a nearby tree. Very few wasps were visible, just one or two crawling on the outside of the nest. We decided to break into the nest to obtain wasp grubs as roach bait, but a natural fear prevented us from making a direct onslaught. After a short discussion it was decided to stuff some burning paper into the nest opening so as to ensure that it was empty of wasps. Within seconds of the burning paper being pushed into the opening the air was full of wasps, thousands of them in a dense cloud! We were lucky to escape serious injury and needless to say we didn't obtain any grubs.

The common wasp (*Vespula vulgaris*) is readily recognised as the unwanted pest at many a picnic. It is aggressive and the sting can be quite painful.

Other members of the wasp family such as *Vespula germanica*, *Vespula rufa* and *Dolichovespula sylvestris* are so like the common wasp that we accept them all as just 'wasps'.

The number of wasps seen during any summer depends on the weather in the early spring. A very cold or wet spring, regardless of later good weather, will result in poor numbers. The reverse is equally true – fine spring weather will result in a virtual plague of these insects later on in the year.

The hornet (*Vespa crabro*) is often mistaken for a common wasp at first sight, especially in the south of England where hornets are relatively common. Full-grown it is bigger than the true wasp, but size is always relative to age and is an unreliable point of identification. When the two insects are seen together and compared, the difference is quite apparent: the hornet is less evenly coloured and has more yellow colour at the rear end; the thorax and head are also darker and often have no yellow markings. Hornets are not nearly as aggressive as wasps and very rarely sting, but when they do the result is much more severe. Many years ago hornets were common insects, but today they have become rather rare, due to the intensive use of insecticides on agricultural land.

The wasp beetle (*Clytus arietis*) is not a member of the wasp family, just an almost perfect imitation. Its appearance is purely protective mimicry for it is completely harmless. In all respects it flies and behaves as a wasp, but on close examination it will be seen that the yellow stripes are much narrower than those of the wasp, and the legs are black instead of yellow.

The longhorn beetle (*Strangalia maculata*) also makes use of the striped yellow-and-black look as a form or protection, but again it is completely harmless. A flying insect that gathers nectar, it is often seen on the wing or trapped by the water, but the long antennae will quickly distinguish it from the wasp.

The digger wasp (*Crabro cribrarius*) is another insect in our 'wasp family'. The name is derived from its nest-building activities in sandy ground. This voracious creature lives on flying insects that are caught on the wing, and often hunts over water. Many of the flies it captures are carried back to the nest where they are stored as food for the growing grubs. Sometimes both digger wasp and prey fall, locked together, to the water surface. The main difference between it and the true wasp is that the head, thorax and legs are all black.

All the above insects could easily be mistaken for common wasps, and all could find themselves on or in the water at various times due to mishap.

When wasps are first trapped by the water-surface film they struggle violently and cause considerable disturbance. However, due to their weight and shell-hard bodies they sink into the surface film very quickly and are then very soon drowned. Although apparently dead, true wasps are still sometimes capable of inflicting their sting; great care should therefore be exercised in handling them for identification purposes.

Fish seem to be oblivious to their stinging tendencies and will take a member of the wasp family at any stage, even when it is obviously alive and kicking.

Most wasp-like insects encountered by the fish are likely to be either wasp beetles or longhorn beetles, especially in the vicinity of birch trees, which are the natural habitat of both species. However, it makes very little difference to the angler which insect he proposes to imitate as they are all so alike in appearance and the well-known yellow-and-black-striped body is common to all.

For many years the American 'McGinty' pattern was the standard fly used to imitate wasps, and quite frankly it deserves the esteem in which it is held; it has a proven record in use. The one fault of this pattern is the difficulty of fishing it semi-submerged in the surface film. If it is not treated with generous amounts of floatant it very quickly becomes waterlogged and sinks quite deep. It is then little better than a yellow and black striped wet fly. If it is treated with floatant the fine chenille body becomes very buoyant and it rides high as a dry fly – neither presentation is ideal, although both will take fish at times as the pattern is so effective.

The writer developed his 'Drone Fly' to overcome this difficulty, but it must be admitted that, to date, it has not proved a more killing pattern than the 'McGinty'.

When the 'McGinty' is well hackled and fished without floatant, and when several false casts are made before each presentation, the fly is inclined to hang down in the water supported by its hackle, and this form of presentation has proved to be very acceptable.

If a small packet of silicone powder (sold under various trade names as a fly floatant), is carried, the fly can be occasionally dipped in the powder to dry it off and to keep the chenille from becoming waterlogged.

Fishing a wasp imitation should be reserved for those very hot, sunny days of midsummer. A short time back the writer was fishing on such a day, and although it was early summer there had been a mini heat-wave for several days with temperatures hovering near 80°F. It was simply gorgeous to be at the waterside, even though trout movement was conspicuous by its absence, there was no sign of any rising fish and none could be spotted in any shady lie. A reasonable number of olive spinners were dancing over the water, some dipping to the water surface, but no interest was being shown by the trout.

Fishing under such conditions is normally considered quite hopeless, but it is, in fact, an ideal time to try a wasp imitation. The water was crystal clear and it seemed a useless tactic to float a 'McGinty' over what appeared to be empty water, but on the third float there was a 'flash' from the stream bed and a good-size trout was visible rising to the fly. It is simply amazing how well camouflaged a trout can be when it hugs the stream bed without throwing a shadow. The incident also showed that such a trout will rise from the bottom providing the water is reasonably shallow, especially if confronted by a substantial terrestrial.

The trout was just over 2 lb, a very good fish under such adverse conditions, and one that would not have been taken on a conventional fly.

It is always difficult to decide what terrestrial pattern to use, and often the nature of the water dictates the choice, but for the hot, sultry days it is very hard to best a wasp imitation fished with a free float in the surface film.

CHAPTER 7

Tying the Wasp Family

It has already been said that we are considering a representation not only of the true wasp, but several insects that sport the familiar yellow and black stripes. For our purpose it is not necessary to differentiate between them – we need only consider how best to obtain the desired effect.

However, there are other aspects to consider besides general coloration. Our imitation must be capable of being presented in a life-like manner, or, to be more precise, in the same manner in which the natural insects behave under similar circumstances. We must also be aware of size, for size has a significant bearing on our success. While it is true that most 'one-off' insects encountered by the trout will vary in size, and selectivity is not expected, weather conditions will affect the acceptance or refusal. We will discuss this problem at length at a later stage.

For years the American 'McGinty' pattern has been in use on both sides of the Atlantic to simulate members of the wasp family, and without doubt it is a very successful pattern at times.

The 'McGinty'

Hook:	12-16 Dry Fly
Body:	Strands of fine black and yellow chenille wound alternately
Tail:	None
Wings:	None
Hackle:	Ginger

Tying the 'McGinty' is very easy. Fig. 8 shows the various stages in winding the separate strands of fine chenille alternately to obtain the striped body. The only difficulty that may be encountered will arise when the two strands of chenille are first tied in. Incorrect tying-in will result in a finished fly with a most peculiar bulbous shape. No difficulty will be experienced if the method that follows is adopted.

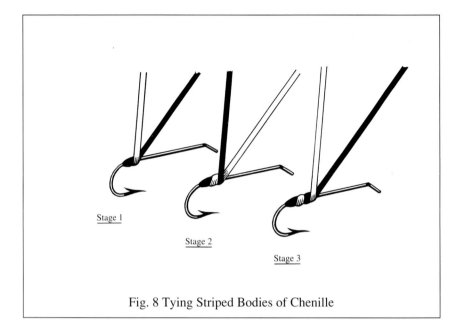

Stage 1

Stage 2

Stage 3

Fig. 8 Tying Striped Bodies of Chenille

All chenille has a twisted thread core, and the fluffy chenille can be easily scraped off this core with the fingernails, leaving the twisted core exposed. Both black and yellow strands should be treated in this manner so that about an inch of core is laid bare. Tie in the exposed core along the hook shank so that the full-bodied chenille starts at the bend of the hook. The first winding of colour is usually yellow, so it is an advantage if the core of the black chenille is left exposed at the bend by ¹⁄₁₆ inch so that it can be laid back towards the hook eye for the yellow strand to be wound over. However, this is only a fly-tying refinement to obtain a better shaped body; a perfectly good 'McGinty' can be tied without bothering to stagger the chenille cores.

It is also a moot point whether it is necessary to make the first stripe yellow, as it is almost certain that the trout will not notice the difference. Very probably the originator of the pattern considered the yellow butt more attractive, or perhaps it was just an accurate copy of the natural insect.

The problem with the 'McGinty' pattern lies in presentation. Most wasp-like insects are 'hard-backed' and not very buoyant in water; they quickly succumb and tend to lie dead in the surface film with the hard, heavy body hanging down submerged. The 'McGinty' does not readily lend itself to this presentation. Treated with a floatant it rides the surface beautifully like a dry fly – quite out of keeping with the type of insect it is supposed to represent. Without floatant it very quickly becomes waterlogged and behaves like a wet fly – equally out of keeping with the naturals.

In the past the 'McGinty' has been used successfully without floatant, but it had to be subjected to continual false casting to dry out the waterlogged chenille body. This explains why results with the 'McGinty' are rather inconsistent, at times taking fish, at other times ignored. Success will depend entirely on the condition of the fly.

The writer's own pattern the 'Drone Fly' was evolved to overcome this difficulty.

Drone Fly

Hook:	12-18 Dry Fly
Body:	Alternate wide stripes of yellow and black – built up by multiple windings of yellow and black tying silk, then clear lacquered several times to a gloss finish
Tail:	None
Wings:	None
Hackle:	Ginger

The advantages of the 'Drone Fly' are numerous. The lacquered hard body will not take up water and a floatant can be used quite freely without having any effect on the body of the fly. The floatant-treated hackle will support the fly at the surface, but the solid body will hang down below the surface most realistically. A further advantage is that the fly can be tied in smaller sizes than chenille will allow.

It must be said the 'Drone Fly', over a period, has not proved any more successful in taking trout than the 'McGinty'. However, it is easier to use, without the chore of continual false casting.

A word of caution. When tying the 'Drone Fly' do not hurry the lacquering process: make sure that each coat of lacquer is completely dry before applying the next coat. Continue the lacquering process until a good gloss results. Using unwaxed tying silk to build up the body will produce a good bright fly.

Now we can consider size. It has been mentioned that size is important, but no explanation was given. Although our imitation represents a variety of yellow and black banded insects of widely differing sizes, it is not this variety that dictates our fly size. The imitation is being presented on a 'one-off' basis and the trout is not feeding selectively. Weather conditions are what create the size problem.

We usually fish our wasp-type imitation during high summer in the brightest conditions, an extremely hot, sunny, sultry day being ideal for our purpose. Under such circumstances trout are usually holed up in shady lies, probably under banks or overhanging foliage. Although the lies may be shady the light is normally very bright. The trout's vision is at its highest level, as it does not have to look directly into dazzling sunlight, yet the brightness in the shade allows every detail to be clearly seen.

It is therefore essential to offer an imitation that lends itself to minimum scrutiny, which means the smaller the better. A large imitation, representing a larger mouthful, might be more tempting, but the fraud will also be more apparent. On another hot day that is cloudy and overcast we might well try a larger imitation as the trout's vision is less acute.

Of course, much of the above is conjecture, but experience has shown that on a particularly bright day a smaller offering is often taken after a larger fly has been refused.

Although terrestrial imitations of all types are very acceptable during high summer, it is the wasp-type imitation that usually accounts for the most fish under extremely bright conditions. In consequence, concealment of the angler becomes of even greater importance than usual when such an imitation is used. Under such bright conditions we are so, so easily seen. Our concealment is even more important than the actual presentation, it cannot be over-emphasised.

CHAPTER 8

Ants

Ants which find themselves on or in the water are looked upon by the trout as staple food. There are basically only four varieties of this insect in the UK which may be encountered by trout, plus a particular fly that falls into the same category for fishing purposes. Even so, two of these ants, being subterranean by nature, are seldom found on or in water except after heavy rainfall. Another, the wood ant (*Formica species*), has a habitat that makes its appearance on water an even rarer event.

So the trout is not often presented with a selection of ants and to be successful the imitation ant should conform to certain requirements that are dictated by these circumstances.

Ants find their way on or into the water in a variety of ways. The subterranean types are often washed into the river or stream by rain. During spate conditions this will be of little interest to the angler, but to the fish they are acceptable together with the multitude of other food forms being swept downstream. It is when light rain in an area upstream has washed such ants into the water that fishing the subterranean ant becomes worthwhile.

Under such conditions an enormous number of ants may be found in the surface film of the water. The only indication to the angler of such a 'slick' of ants may be the number of sipping rises taking place. Close examination of the water surface will explain why the ants are not immediately apparent: they will all be semi-submerged and carried along by the current just below the surface film.

The colour of ants varies, and subterranean ants washed into the water may be black, brown or red. The common black ant (*Lasius niger*) can also be a flying species, and on warm days in late summer it swarms in vast numbers. Mating takes place in the air on the wing, and after mating only the females survive to lay eggs: the males quickly die. Dead or 'spent' males may well fall to the water in large numbers and are much appreciated by the waiting trout.

An insect often mistaken for a flying black ant is the sepsid fly (*Sepsis cynipsea*). It looks very similar to a black ant, but a close examination will reveal that the ends of the wings are spotted. Sepsid flies swarm over vegetation in vast numbers and can be found on the water in the same way as ants. To the angler, and the trout, there is little difference between these insects.

Any red or brown ants that are encountered will be either mound ants (*Lasius flavus*) or the red ant (*Myrmica rubra*). Both are quite small, ¼–⅜ inch in length, and being subterranean in habit they are not as often seen as the black ants which are much more active above ground. The red ant can sting, the only UK ant with this ability.

Ants abound from March to October, the late summer being the most active time, and from what has been said it will be seen that they are ideal terrestrials to imitate. However, fishing an ant imitation does require a special approach. Some anglers are extremely successful, while others experience no success at all: it depends entirely on the presentation technique.

If very small red, brown or black ant imitations are used they must be fished as a 'wet fly' just below the surface of the water. To avoid any unnatural movement it is better than an upstream cast is made. In fact, fishing to simulate these little drowned ants requires a similar technique to that used when fishing the nymph.

Flying ants and sepsid flies require a different approach, and here the skills of the angler familiar with fishing an imitation spent spinner of the mayfly type flies, are most useful. As well as being found in or on the water for various reasons, flying black ants also swarm and dance in the air in such vast numbers that many automatically find themselves touching the water surface during their gyrations, and having touched the water they are trapped in the surface film. There they struggle to get free and consequently attract the attention of nearby trout. On other occasions the males fall 'spent' to the water surface after mating. 'Spent' ants are inanimate insects with wings outspread and are just carried along by the current. Due to their lack of buoyancy both the 'spent' and trapped drowned ants will sink to just below the surface film. Other black ants, winged or otherwise, will be washed into the water during rain.

So it becomes clear that the winged black ant imitation may be fished dry as a 'spent' fly, or twitched on the water surface to simulate a trapped insect. Or, on the other hand, it may be fished wet, being cast upstream to obtain a free drift similar in style to nymph fishing. Possibly the most productive of these methods is to simulate the 'spent' insect.

It must be remembered that the 'spent' black ant or sepsid fly is either dead or dying, and will be swept along by the current while lying in the surface film of the water with wings outspread. No manipulation to simulate movement is required by the angler. The technique of a good presentation is no different from that used by the angler fishing the dry fly, (spinner): in both cases extreme care is needed to avoid drag and, of course, the cast should be upstream.

The use of an ant imitation is preferable to a standard 'spent' fly of the mayfly type when there are no 'spent' spinners on the water. Fish are opportunists where feeding is concerned, but are wary of single unexpected flies, whereas the odd terrestrial is accepted. Chance prospecting, when no obvious flies are on the water, calls for a terrestrial pattern.

Although colours of ants vary from red through brown to black, it has been observed that an alien colour is often more attractive to the fish. Due to the hard glossy bodies of these insects, it may well be that other colours are reflected and the fish do not always see them as we do. It is also a fact that black is not a true colour. This is easily demonstrated if artists' black oil colours are diluted – the result can vary between purple and silver-grey. Certainly it has been shown over and over again that an ant imitation does not have to be black to interest fish. Colour will be discussed at greater length when we come to tie the imitations.

Although convinced of the value of ant imitations, the writer went through a period of extreme frustration regarding them. Trout were observed taking 'spent' black ants, but efforts to offer an imitation brought poor results. If I had not known that other anglers were extremely successful with the ant, I would have given it up as a bad job. During this period of frustration I tied some peculiar ant imitations, varied size considerably, used many different materials and tried a whole variety of colours – sometimes extreme primary colours such as yellow and bright red.

As a result of the above experimentation a rather amusing incident took place. A nice-sized trout was observed taking 'spent' black ants whilst in a safe lie close to the bank under overhanging foliage. It was a difficult place to cast to. Nevertheless a standard 'spent' black ant was nicely presented, but totally ignored. A similar fly, but coloured bright yellow, was then offered, and again no interest was shown.

In the fly-box were three extremely large 'spent' ants coloured bright pillar-box red, very garish in appearance, purely the result of idle time spent at the tying bench. One of these monstrosities was duly tied to the tippet and a cast made. Perhaps it was due to the difference in size, but the cast was completely bungled and the fly lost in the overhanging foliage. A second monstrosity was mounted and another cast made with exactly the same result, except that this time the fly was lost among some foliage to the rear. In utter despair the last of the red trio was taken from the fly-box and cast to the visible trout. This time the fly reached the water, just at the right point, but the leader was nicely looped over the lower overhanging branches.

Before anything could be done to rectify the situation the red monstrosity was firmly taken by the trout. The trout pulled one way, the caught up leader pulled another, the result was inevitable.

It is hard to say if anything can actually be learned from the incident. It would appear that size is of little importance providing the shape is correct. It would also seem that colour is of little consequence, but on reflection this might not be so. The high gloss given to the body shape must reflect in the sun and perhaps the underlying colour is not all that apparent. The presentation described was, by pure chance, near perfect, with almost no tippet on the water and with the most delicate of landings. If anything is to be learned, it is probably that presentation is far more important than the fly itself, especially where the single odd ant is involved.

CHAPTER 9

Tying the Ant

There are a number of tying patterns already established for the ant, as the value of this insect has been appreciated for many years. It is not suggested that these patterns are of little use, or that the writer's patterns are vastly superior; it is only intended to offer observations on what has been gleaned from much time spent on experimentation.

Existing ant patterns range from tiny red ants tied with horse hair or monofilament nylon dyed the appropriate colour, to large winged and hackled patterns with dubbed or herl bodies. Despite all this innovation the ant, as a fly pattern, has never really come up to expectation considering the trout's penchant for this insect.

I said earlier that I had experienced intense frustration with this insect, and only occasional successes encouraged further experimentation. It has always been obvious that sooner or later good results would be obtained if the artificial could be improved. Fish very rarely ignore the natural insect – only our imitations!

Time and again it was realised that the problems were only partly with the imitation; by far the most important criterion was the presentation. In fact, the lack of knowledge as to how the natural insect behaved when in or on the water, plus its appearance to the fish, were the main stumbling points.

It must be appreciated that a flying ant, the usually presented pattern, must be fished as a dead 'spent' insect in the surface film, just as any 'spent' *Ephemeroptera* pattern is presented. However, there are important differences to be taken into account if the presentation is to appear right to the fish. Firstly the ant must be semi-submerged as this is not a floating insect, secondly the body must not be translucent, and thirdly the body must be capable of strong reflection.

If we ponder these points it quickly becomes apparent that some existing patterns fall short of our requirements, the reasons for our failures become clearer.

Another point, not as important but nevertheless requiring attention, is that the ant has truly gossamer wings. Hard, opaque feather material can never realistically portray such wings, and the omission of wings and their replacement by a hackle is a mistake. A 'hackle only' fly is intended to give a 'buzzy' effect of wing movement, and remember in this case that our presentation is intended to represent a dead 'spent' insect.

So slowly we build up a picture of what is required of an ant pattern, and can settle to the task of incorporating these points at the tying bench.

The 'Spent' Flying Ant

Hook:	16 or 18 Long Shank dry fly
Tying Silk:	Usually black
Hackle:	Dark ginger
Wings:	Polywing – double strand

The Polywing material is the only material that, so far, has been found acceptable in use. Without doubt other materials will do a similar job, but none have so far been discovered. Polywing is obtainable from Sportfish Ltd of Hay-on-Wye, Powys.

Our first consideration must be to body shape, and Fig. 9 shows this in detail. The body, thorax and head are built up with tying silk, and here a few tips may be useful. No attempt should be made to build up the shape quickly with a heavy coarse thread, as this will result in a very distorted fly. Patience is required: a fine tying silk will slowly build up to an excellent outline that will lend itself to later glazing with cellulose varnish.

The colour of the tying silk is a vexing question. Obviously black is the first choice, and probably the best, but other colours have also proved effective. We are up against the problem of reflection, plus the underlying colour of black which can vary. It is believed that, in a strong light, the fish may well see an underlying colour in the natural that is not apparent to us and is beyond our understanding. All that can be said is that ant imitations of bright red and yellow have, in the past, proved very attractive to trout, and their use should not be lightly dismissed.

Once the body shape has been obtained it should be glazed before any further tying takes place. The first step is to apply a black cellulose to the bound shape, using a fine dubbing needle. Again, patience is required, as this coat of black cellulose must be completely dry before proceeding. The final step is a coat of clear cellulose over the black, applied in the same way. If coloured silk has been used instead of black, then the appropriate coloured cellulose can be used as a first coat. No further tying can take place until the cellulose is completely dry and hard.

The fly is completed by tying in the wing at the waist as shown in Fig. 9 and afterwards a sparse hackle – no more than two turns to represent the legs.

Polywing is an easy material to use for winging, as all fibres are continuous and very straight. Although it appears to be limp when it is in a long continuous length, once tied in and cut off the wings will be found to be rather rigid and inclined to splay out in a very natural manner. Being a synthetic it will not take up water, nor

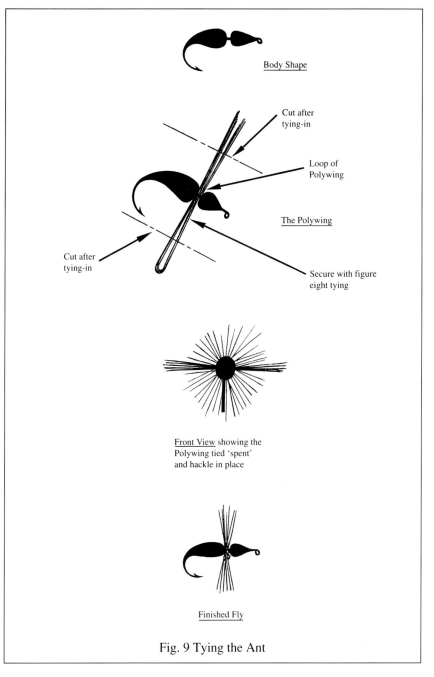

Body Shape

Cut after
tying-in

Loop of
Polywing

The Polywing

Cut after
tying-in

Secure with figure
eight tying

Front View showing the
Polywing tied 'spent'
and hackle in place

Finished Fly

Fig. 9 Tying the Ant

does it need a floatant. One method is to draw a length of Polywing through moistened fingers before tying in; the wet material is then much easier to handle and dries out very quickly.

Various forms of smaller non-flying ants may be tied in the same manner as detailed above, of course with the wings omitted. The hackle is always necessary to represent the legs. These smaller imitations may be tied down to a size 26 hook, and the construction will give no difficulty in such small sizes.

The colour of these minute ants is also a matter of conjecture, as an added dimension of difficulty occurs in their use. Although these small imitations can be fished in the surface film it is far better if they are fished sub-surface, for in practice it is extremely difficult to get the necessarily fine tippit to sink and for the fly to appear unattached. When fished sub-surface the fly will always reflect the rocks, stones, gravel or plant life in the vicinity, and it is open to conjecture which colour will give the most natural-looking appearance to the fish.

Some years ago the writer evolved the Reflector Nymph, a nymph designed to obtain the utmost reflection of its surroundings in a truly translucent manner. The effectiveness of the Reflector Nymph has been proved beyond question, so this reflective capability must be fully taken into account as it applies to the glossy ant.

The faceted gold construction of the Reflector Nymph cannot be used for the ant, but it is possible to achieve similar results from a light amber colour that will reflect the sombre browns and greens that are found sub-surface. Primrose tying silk that has been treated with spirit varnish will give such a colour.

The procedure is quite simple. The usual coat of coloured cellulose is not given; instead the spirit varnish is used, then, when completely dry, the final gloss of clear cellulose is applied in the usual way.

The results may be imaginary, but the added confidence in the fly is well worth having, as confidence while fishing induces a more expectant attitude with increased concentration.

CHAPTER 10

Moths

After the summer evening rise is over and the sun has set, there comes that peculiar time of quarter light commonly referred to as dusk. In truth the light has completely gone, but our eyes have become accustomed to the gloom and we can still see the water clearly. It is an interesting fact that if we are indoors it appears quite dark outside, but if we are still by the water the light is sufficient to carry on fishing.

As the gloom deepens it becomes the time to fish sedge or moth imitations. In these pages we are not concerned with aquatic sedges, only with the terrestrial moths, but there is a marked similarity in the way the imitations are presented, and often either pattern will bring the same results.

All moths belong to the order *Lepidoptera*, but not all are terrestrial in the true sense of the word. It is not commonly known that several moths are aquatic by nature, but this is indeed so, and their larval life is completely sub-aquatic. The aquatic moths mostly belong to the separate *Pyralidae* family; however, the adult insects may be classed as terrestrial for our purposes as we are not interested in the hatching moth, only in the adult insect that may be found on or in the water. In this respect there is no difference between the truly terrestrial and the aquatic species.

The use of moth imitations has always been a haphazard operation for the majority of anglers. In fact some writers have even suggested that a general pattern in brown or white, tied on various size hooks, will suffice in most circumstances. It might well be true that such an approach will catch the odd fish, but it certainly does not satisfy the discerning angler who would like to have a little more confidence in the fly he is using. Not all moths are active at the same time of the year and their coloration and form varies to a marked degree. To be truly effective the moth pattern needs to be selected with the same care as any other fly.

It will be of some help to anglers seeking to identify moths, or trying to decide on a suitable pattern at a certain time of the year, if we list the most common moths seen on the water and the months of the year in which they are most active. Of course, this can only be taken as a very general guide; various weather conditions, temperatures etc, have a great bearing on their nocturnal activities.

If we also specify whether the moth is 'small', 'medium' or 'large', it will assist in selecting a suitable imitative pattern. We can designate as follows:

$$1–1\tfrac{1}{4} \text{ inch} \quad = \quad \text{S}$$
$$1\tfrac{1}{4}–1\tfrac{1}{2} \text{ inch} \quad = \quad \text{M}$$
$$1\tfrac{1}{2} \text{ inch } + \quad = \quad \text{L}$$

A further specification will note if the imitation should be dressed 'fat' or 'thin', (F or T). This designation refers to the body of the insect, which in some cases is quite fat and furry and in others quite slim and smooth.

Not very scientific! However, for anglers wishing to select an appropriate artificial, the above descriptions, plus the coloration, will lead to the correct final selection.

Before discussing the various common moths in detail it is necessary to refer to two insects in particular. The first is not a moth, but a butterfly of the family *Hesperiidae*, which are known as skippers.

The large skipper (*Ochlodes venata*) could very easily be mistaken for a small moth. At times it is active during the day, but it is also semi-nocturnal in habit and very attracted by water reflection. The natural habitat is over waterside meadows, and it is easily identified by a wildly erratic darting flight. The colour is a distinctive golden brown. The most active months are usually June and July. (Designation: S and F.)

The other insect referred to above is a true moth that is often seen near or on water. The burnet (*Zygaena filipendulae*) is easily identified by the large vivid red spots on the wings. The natural habitat is over marshlands and low-lying meadows and it is very slow in flight. Although sometimes in or on the water from May to August, it is of no interest to the fish due to a distasteful yellow poisonous fluid secreted in the body. Fish and birds are perhaps warned off by the vivid colouring, or perhaps by some past bad experience, and it is useless fishing an imitation of this moth.

Often anglers will refer to moths as 'ghost moth' or 'swift moth', and will also use these names to describe the artificial patterns. Perhaps the ghost swift moth (*Hepialus humuli*) is the root of this confusion, as it is one of the most common moths in the UK. The male and female of the species differ considerably in appearance and size and it would be an easy mistake to assume that there were two species, then to split up the name accordingly.

Hepialus humuli is a very primitive moth which is unable to feed as an adult. It is large, some $1\tfrac{3}{4}–3$ inches in size, but the male is much smaller than the female. While the male has shiny white wings and could be grouped with other white moths that are nocturnal fliers, the large female is a lovely pale golden yellow insect with a large furry head. The species are easily identified, as at sunset the male makes a very slow, undulating flight over vegetation to attract the female for mating. The active period is during June, July and August. (Designation: male M and F, female L and F.)

The white ermine (*Spilosoma lubricipeda*) that is usually active during May and June is a ready nocturnal flier that is very attracted to water. Many fly patterns exist for this moth, as together with the common white wave (*Cabera pusaria*), it is the 'white moth' held in such high esteem by night anglers.

The white ermine is a larger moth than the common white wave, and it is also more yellow in appearance with very small brown spots. The common white wave is active from May right through to August; it is very nocturnal by nature and also very attracted to water. So it becomes apparent why a yellowish white moth pattern in various sizes, fished at dusk during May to August, has become a good choice for anglers. (Designations: S and L, also F.)

The brimstone moth (*Opisthograptis luteolata*) is another largely nocturnal insect with a natural habitat among woodlands. As dusk falls it becomes very active, flying among the trees, swooping down to any nearby water surface where it is often temporarily trapped in the surface film. This moth is particularly active from April to August, and sometimes is inclined towards daytime flying during high summer, mostly on very sunny mornings. The coloration is yellow with brown markings on the wings. (Designation: M and T.)

The green oak moth (*Tortrix viridana*), will very often make nocturnal flights, but it is only really active during June and July. The natural habitat is among oak trees, and it is always easily identified by its brilliant green colour. (Designation: S and T.)

The green oak caterpillar is small by moth standards and completely green. Massive numbers of these caterpillars are extremely active among foliage and very often fall from the leaves, and perhaps to water below. The standard pattern of 'Green Caterpillar' so often offered for sale is probably based on this larva.

In Canada and the USA the Green Caterpillar is called an Inch Worm, and the pattern is the same as that used in the UK. The writer recalls some fabulous fishing in Ontario when the Inch Worm accounted for large numbers of excellent fish. However, although the Inch Worm was such a popular pattern, there did not seem to be much interest among anglers in the adult moth. It was a popular theory that 'something large, bushy and black' was needed for successful night fishing. It is a pity that the writer had no opportunity to study the local moths – some spectacular sport might have been the result.

The yellow shell moth (*Camptogramma bilineata*) is another moth active during June and July. The natural habitat is over meadows and fields and although often seen on the wing during the day, it is also a confirmed nocturnal flier. The colour is predominantly yellow, but there are some brown markings on the wings. (Designation: S and T.)

A large moth that is also active during June and July is the large emerald (*Geometra papilionaria*), another nocturnal flier. It is common among woodlands, and at dusk will be found swooping among birch, hazel or beech trees. At first sight this moth could be mistaken for a butterfly as the general form is very similar. The coloration is a greeny white. (Designation: L and F.)

The china marks moth (*Nymphula nymphaeata*), has been left to the last as it is not a true terrestrial, but one of the aquatic moths mentioned earlier. The natural habitat of the adult insect is on riverside vegetation and foliage. The eggs are laid on water plants and the larval and pupae stages are sub-aquatic. The adult moth is active from June to August, mostly at night, but daytime flying is not unknown. The coloration is a mottled brown and white. (Designation: S and T.)

It is quite common for moths to be on the water surface from dusk onwards. No matter how dark the night may appear to us there is always some light, and water surfaces are reflected. Reflection is amplified by light, and a very light night will intensify the reflection. The attraction to moths is obviously the reflected light, and they fly to the water surface in the same manner as they would to a well-lit window.

Moths are seldom trapped by the water – they are very strong fliers and are usually able to break loose from the surface film. Often they skim over the water surface during 'take-off', causing quite a disturbance. Without doubt this disturbance is very attractive to fish and the result is often a noisy, splashy rise.

There is an added attraction to fishing a moth imitation when the light has faded: it can easily be seen on the water, not only by the fish – but by the angler as well. It is surprising how well large flies can be seen in poor light on a reflective surface such as water, and it is always easier to strike a rise that can be seen rather than felt.

In practice it has been found that the common problem of drag can be ignored when fishing a moth. The best fishing procedure is to treat the moth imitation generously with floatant, then to cast as a dry fly to likely lies. As soon as the fly alights on the water surface, impart movement by retrieving in short pulls, but take care not to allow the fly to become waterlogged. It is often a wise precaution to give all moth patterns several treatments of floatant before leaving home, allowing the fly to dry out thoroughly between treatments.

The writer remembers a beautiful brown trout that took a moth imitation when the line was being reeled in fast to end a day's fishing. The fly was skimming over the water surface like a miniature motor boat and the wake of the pursuing trout was something to behold! So be prepared for very hard takes when fishing the moth, and be sure your tippet strength is up to the job in hand.

CHAPTER 11

Tying the Moths

A general moth pattern, usually called the 'great white moth', has been around for a number of years, but little attempt has been made truly to represent the moths which are commonly found on or in water.

Looking through the professional tiers lists and illustrations often leaves the impression that they have no real idea of what is needed. In fact, one very well-known tackle house offers a moth imitation with the description 'Moth – these are blown on to the water', then goes on to illustrate the offered moth imitation with a photograph of a representation of the burnet moth (*Zygaena filipendulae*) – a poisonous moth that is not attractive to fish. Worse, the listed moth imitation is recommended for use from May to September, which is not in keeping with the active period of the burnet moth – even supposing you wanted to fish such a pattern.

All of this is not at all helpful to the serious angler, so if good moth patterns are to be fished they will obviously have to be home-tied. Of course, the future may bring an improvement to the scene, with the professional tiers taking a greater interest, but in the meantime let us consider what we can do to help ourselves.

The late Richard Walker evolved a moth pattern which he called the 'Ghost Swift Moth'. Obviously a great deal of thought had gone into the design, and Richard Walker wrote that the pattern would serve to imitate a number of white or pale-coloured moths. It was a good beginning, and Richard Walker used the pattern for many years with very little variation.

It is intended in these pages to enlarge the scope of patterns available, and to draw on the writer's past experience to present to the discerning angler good imitation patterns that can be fished with confidence. At the same time different methods of tying will be discussed, methods which have proved in practice to give the best results.

We have previously looked at nine moths that are commonly found on or in the water at dusk. Considering the colour of each, plus the designation that was given to each insect, we find that four patterns will serve to imitate all of them.

The new 'Great White Moth' pattern will represent the white ermine, the common white wave, the large emerald and the male ghost swift. Although the common white wave is usually smaller than the others, a size 12 hook will suffice for all four. The problem of colour variation should not be taken too seriously. The slight differences between white, yellow–white and greeny white, can be ignored by all except the true purist, especially when the fly is to be presented in a poor light. Size, shape and general impression are more important than colour in this instance.

The large skipper, the brimstone and the yellow shell can be jointly represented by a smaller, similar pattern that is yellow in colour. At times the writer prefers a more distinct and separate pattern for the large skipper, especially if goodly numbers of the insect are on the wing, and this separate pattern will be given for general information.

A further small but similar pattern in green is required to represent the green oak moth, and a further small distinctive pattern for the china marks moth.

Considerable experimentation has taken place to evolve patterns for these moths, and over a period of time ideas have changed. Earlier writings have described patterns that have since progressed in the light of experience gained. Of course, fly-pattern design is constantly changing and no apology is needed for that. No fly pattern is ever the ultimate – we must always try to improve.

The original moth pattern by the late Richard Walker is illustrated and fully described, for this pattern is the base design from which the new patterns have evolved.

Ghost Swift Moth (Richard Walker)

Hook:	8 Long Shank
Body:	Cream Ostrich herl – tied fat
Rib:	A stiff-fibred cream cock hackle
Wings:	A large bunch of Swan secondary feather fibres – tied flat
Hackle:	One cream and one pale ginger cock hackle
Silk:	White

The only variation made over the years by Richard Walker was to lengthen the wing and to cut it off more square. There is no doubt that this is a fine base pattern for the 'Great White Moth', and only slight changes have suggested themselves during long practical use.

The Great White Moth
(ghost swift, white ermine, white wave and large emerald moths)

Hook:	10 or 12 Long Shank
Body:	Dressed fat with tying silk, then covered with white feather fibre cut from Swan secondary feathers
Rib:	A cream hackle – tied palmer
Wings:	White hair – tied flat as a bunch then separated into two wings and cut off square just beyond bend of hook
Silk:	White

No difficulty will be experienced tying the feather fibre body if double strands of fibre are tied in as required during the dressing, i.e. starting at the bend it may take three separate windings to complete the full length of the body. It will also strengthen the fly if the built-up silk body is treated with clear cellulose varnish, then the feather fibre wound on while the varnish is still wet. The wing of hair is tied in flat, 'streamer/bucktail style', then separated into separate wings with figure-of-eight turns of silk before the ends are cut off square. Suitable hair is bleached grey squirrel tail, bleached goat hair, or best of all polar bear. Polar bear hair is a superlative material for this purpose, the texture is just perfect. Unfortunately few readers will be able to use it, due to a necessary ban on this material. However, if your tying kit still contains some polar bear hair, it could not be put to a better use. See Fig. 10.

The above 'Great White Moth' pattern can, with variations, be used as the basic design for the next two patterns required.

Yellow Moth
(brimstone, yellow shell and large skipper)

Hook:	12 or 14 Long Shank
Body:	Dressed slim with tying silk then covered with yellow feather fibre cut from Swan secondary feather
Rib:	A yellow cock hackle – tied palmer
Wings:	Yellow hair tied flat as a bunch and separated into separate wings, then cut off square just beyond the bend of the hook
Silk:	Primrose

An alternative pattern for the large skipper has decided advantages when this insect is known to be flying in the vicinity in large numbers.

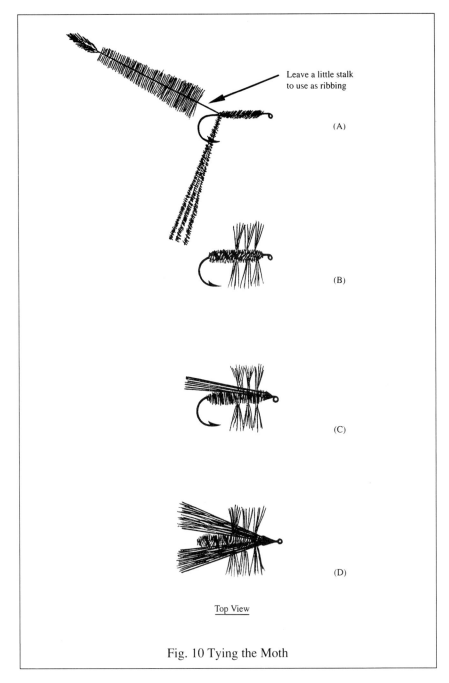

Leave a little stalk
to use as ribbing

(A)

(B)

(C)

(D)

Top View

Fig. 10 Tying the Moth

Large Skipper

Hook: 14 Long Shank
Body: Dressed fat with tying silk, then covered with yellow feather fibre
Rib: Gold mylar tinsel under a yellow cock hackle tied palmer
Wings: Deep yellow hair tied flat as a bunch and separated into two wings, then cut off square just beyond bend of hook
Silk: Yellow

The china marks moth is not truly represented by any of the above patterns. Some anglers have a high regard for this insect, others prefer to ignore it and fish the large white patterns. It is probably true to say that many fish taken on brown sedge patterns took the fly as a representation of a china marks moth. As this moth frequently flies at dusk and after dark, it is bound to be on the water at the same time as the sedges. Perhaps the best approach is to fish a brown sedge pattern – one with a particularly pale-coloured wing of mottled turkey feather. Certainly the writer has not evolved a specific pattern that is any better.

Moth patterns need to be extremely good floaters so that they can be skittered over the water surface without becoming waterlogged. A very good way to obtain this skittering action is to allow the fly to travel downstream, below the angler, then to hold a tight line while the fly travels across the current in an arc, causing a slight wake.

The construction of feather-fibre body and hair wing certainly helps in this respect, but it is still necessary to treat them thoroughly with a floatant. The best treatment found, so far, is to use Permafloat to which a good blob of Gink has been added. If the bottle of Permafloat is well shaken the Gink will dissolve into the mixture without difficulty. If treatment is given at home rather than at the water's edge, several dips can be given and each allowed to dry thoroughly.

At one time the writer tied many moth patterns with spun deer-hair bodies (Muddler Minnow style). When close cropped the bodies give a nice impression of being furry, and the deer hair added to the floatability. Experience gained in use indicated that coloured feather-fibre bodies were more attractive to the fish, so slowly and reluctantly the deer-hair bodies were superseded. However, spun deer hair has so many advantages that the writer still uses the material for the bodies of brown sedge imitations.

The use of feather fibre as a material for bodies was first brought to the notice of the fly-tying fraternity by Richard Walker as long ago as 1974, although it is not known if he was the originator of the idea. Richard Walker stated that the material combined neatness with translucency, and that when viewed against the light the colour was still available. The original suggestion was that the fibre strands be twisted together to form a 'rope' before winding on, and that a double thickness winding be used to obtain fatter bodies. In practice the twisting into a 'rope' was found partially to destroy the 'furry' effect, and double thickness windings became very easily unravelled when subjected to the teeth of trout.

The use of untwisted double or treble strands of fibre, wound on together over a built up body of silk that is wet with varnish, has proved completely satisfactory in use. It is a fine material for moth imitations and is thoroughly recommended.

CHAPTER 12

Crane Flies

It has long been appreciated by those anglers who fish the reservoirs that the so-called 'Daddy Longlegs' is an effective surface lure for still-water trout. Some years back the late Richard Walker wrote at length on the still-water technique, and evolved a pattern that was successful when fished as a dry fly. He appreciated that every 'Daddy' on the water surface was not dead, and advised the twitching of the fly from time to time. The Irish have also used live 'Daddies' for many years when dapping on the large Irish loughs, so there is no doubt whatever that fish are attracted to this fly.

The technique required for river fishing has been less appreciated, and more work is required on the generally accepted pattern if the full potential is to be realised. Large cruising rainbows or browns of still-water may well be tempted by a chunky mouthful on the water directly in their path, but the real 'Daddy' is a very delicate insect and a good imitation is required if a wild river trout, on feeding station, is to be deceived.

The 'Daddy' is a crane fly which belongs to the order *Diptera*, and is of the *Tipulidae* family of flies. There are vast numbers of these flies and many varieties, some 12,000 varieties are known worldwide. In the UK we are mainly concerned with two that lend themselves to terrestrial lures for trout. Both of these are very common, but differ considerably in appearance, colour and shape.

The crane fly (*Tipula maxima*), is quite large, 1¼–1¾ inches in length when fully adult, and we are forced to consider the immature insect or young adult for imitative purposes. The natural habitat is woodlands, usually close to water, and eggs are laid in very moist soil or directly into very shallow water. The colour of the crane fly is a sandy brown with mottled pale brown wings. Prominent features are a long, extremely thin, segmented body, an obviously large thorax and, of course, the very long, fragile legs. This fly is active from April to August, but is most obvious during high summer when it is a full adult.

The common crane fly (*Tipula paludosa*), is a very different fly. It is smaller than *Tipula maxima*, being only ¾–1 inch long as an adult. It is active from July to September and the natural habitat is over grasslands. Eggs are laid in soil and the hatched larvae often cause considerable damage to farm crops. The coloration is a light yellow, and although it has a general 'Daddy' appearance the body is considerably thicker than that of *Tipula maxima*, and the thorax very much more pronounced. The wings are also much shorter.

All crane flies are very clumsy walkers and inclined to stay quite stationary when not on the wing. When not actually flying they may be seen in large numbers just sitting on vegetation. The legs are extremely delicate and are easily broken off – apparently with no ill effect to the fly!

The wings are quite long and narrow, and only two are readily visible. As a matter of fact they have four wings, but the second pair have evolved to balancing organs and are not very easily seen. In repose the wings are carried at varying angles in an effort to balance the fly, but with little effect as 'Daddies' are blown about even by the gentlest breeze.

Once the 'Daddy' has been blown to the water surface it cannot become airborne again, and the fine delicate legs fail to support the fly and quickly penetrate the surface film. The fly faces a quick death by drowning and the rapid movement of its wings only causes a slight twitching of the elongated body. Very soon the fly is lying in the surface film fully 'spent' with its legs trailed out behind it. It depends entirely on the surface turbulence of the water whether it is carried along by the current as a 'spent' fly in the surface film, or as a 'drowned' insect below the surface.

Our 'Daddy' imitation may therefore be fished either as a 'spent' dry fly or a 'drowned' wet fly; the nature of the water flow will indicate to us the best approach.

Experience has proved that a sunken 'Daddy' in free drift is an extremely effective wet fly. It obviously offers a larger outline than a traditional wet fly, and the long legs trailing in the current perhaps excite the fish to take. Only when the water surface is smooth and unbroken is it worth considering the use of a dry 'spent' imitation.

The only difficulty in using the 'Daddy' as a wet fly lies in getting such a flimsy fly to sink. The construction of a 'Daddy' imitation does not lend itself to the age-old practice of rubbing the fly into some mud, and sinkant preparations made from Fuller's Earth tend to gum-up the legs. A split shot is out of the question for such a lightweight fly. Quite a problem. Two false casts and we are back to a floater!

Solutions to problems are sometimes so obvious that we fail to see them. If you carry a small bottle of glycerine and dip the fly into it now and again it will sink like a stone immediately it touches the water.

An upstream cast, to obtain a free drift, is the ideal way to fish the wet 'Daddy'. Any trace of drag should be avoided, and certainly no attempt made to manipulate or retrieve the fly. Perhaps because of the illusion of size, created by the trailing legs, the imitation is rarely gently taken. In practice it has not been found necessary to watch very closely for slight movements of line or leader. Generally speaking the take is felt as the total fly is engulfed by a moving fish, only a tightening of the line is necessary to set the hook.

The writer used to fish a small mountain stream in Wales where the trout, although on the small side, were the most beautifully coloured wild brownies ever seen. The water was not really suitable for dry-fly work, but a wet fly produced reasonable results. It was a wet 'Daddy' that really succeeded with fish often being taken on consecutive casts.

While the crane fly is the better pattern to fish 'dry', the common crane fly is better for wet fly fishing in running water. Perhaps the coloration of dull yellow is more easily seen by the fish, but more likely it is the bulkier outline that is the added attraction. Fish feeding sub-surface are generally bolder and more voracious, and will not willingly pass up what appears to be a substantial titbit.

The imitation 'Daddy' is not an easy fly to tie, but is worth every moment of the time it takes to construct, and every effort to improve the pattern is very well rewarded.

CHAPTER 13

Tying the 'Daddy Longlegs'

It must be stated at the outset that any 'Daddy' pattern is a time-consuming fly to tie, whether it is one of the several well-known versions or the new patterns that follow. However, the value of this fly is such that every minute spent in the tying is rewarded many times over.

Before we consider the actual tying it would be as well if we reviewed what is currently on offer to us and what is generally regarded as a 'Daddy' pattern.

Due in large part to the thoughtful approach of the late Richard Walker, the 'Daddy' imitation has largely been accepted by still-water anglers. The acceptance of the insect itself raised no problem as it has been in use as a natural bait when dapping for many years – the use of an artificial was the only innovation. It was quickly found that, under the right conditions, the artificial was also a good producer of fish, but this fact requires closer examination.

The various commercially tied offerings, although having a general 'Daddy' appearance, fall far short of a really good imitation of the natural. There is no doubt, however, that these patterns are successful on still-water, so let us consider why this is so. We all know that a bulky Muddler Minnow fished in the surface film of still-water often brings spectacular results, so we should not be that surprised if a rather bulky 'Daddy' on the surface also attracts attention. Sedge flies and moths, often heavily over-dressed, also produce well at times. It is a phenomenon of still-water that large, cruising fish are very often attracted by a substantial morsel that lies in their path in the surface film, especially if the water surface is choppy and the food objects are in wind-lanes. However, none of these circumstances or conditions are of much help to the river angler fishing the dry patterns – a different technique entirely.

The natural crane fly is an extremely delicate insect, and we must accept at the outset that the fly-tying materials available to us make true imitation almost impossible. We must therefore concentrate on representing the main features of the fly, those that are obviously recognition points to the fish.

Firstly let us consider the body of the insect, and its relation to the hook. Hooks with extra long shanks which carry dubbed feather fibre or quill bodies, cannot

Ground Beetle Imitation

Chafer Beetle Imitation

Common Green Grasshopper Imitation

Leaf Hopper Imitation

Wasp Imitation

Ant Imitation

Ghost Swift Moth Imitation
(R. Walker)

White Moth Imitation

Yellow Moth Imitation

*Crane Fly Imitation
(Dry Pattern)*

*Crane Fly Imitation
(Wet Pattern)*

Large Midge Imitation

Small Midge Imitation

Black Gnat Imitation

*Green Oak Moth
Caterpillar Imitation*

Buff-Tip Caterpillar Imitation

truly represent the wraithlike 'Daddy' required for dry-fly presentation on running water. The hook needs to be a standard long-shank dry-fly hook about size 16, so of necessity we must consider tying the fly with a detached body, or something similar. We must also use a body material that can be tied in this manner yet adequately represent the extremely thin body of a natural 'Daddy'. Furthermore it must float well. After much experimentation it was found that deer hair-fibres, bound by ribbing then tied in flat, achieved the criteria required above.

The legs of the 'Daddy' are best represented by pheasant-tail fibres that have been knotted along their length. Some credit must go to Richard Walker for this innovation, and for his suggestions of knotting each fibre twice and tying in sloping backwards. It is only necessary to add that the number of legs is not important – trout cannot count! – and one or two extra will compensate for those lost while the fly is in use.

Another important feature of the crane fly is the very pronounced thorax, and artificials should clearly produce this illusion at the base of the wings.

We can now discuss two patterns which will represent *Tipula maxima* for fishing 'dry' and *T. paludosa* for 'wet' work sub-surface. The tyings are somewhat different as the flies themselves differ in appearance; materials also need to be varied according to the fishing method used.

Crane Fly (Dry) – Tipula Maxima

Hook:	16 or 18 Standard Dry Fly
Body:	15-20 long strands of natural deer hair tied in flat and ribbed with tying silk
Thorax:	Built up with tying silk
Legs:	6-8 pheasant-tail fibres knotted twice in their length and tied in sloping back
Wings:	Cree hackle points
Hackle:	Cree or light ginger
Silk:	Brown

Fig. 11 shows the above tying in detail. After the hook has been prepared by carefully wrapping with tying silk along the complete shank (A), the body is prepared by selecting about 15–20 deer-hair fibres (B), then wetting them with golden gum so they matt together (C). It is then a simple matter to rib with tying silk (D). In practice it has been found that tying each rib separately (three to four tyings) was quicker and easier.

The ribbed deer-hair body is then whipped to the hook shank and the end cut off square, as shown in (E). Pheasant-tail fibre legs are now prepared and tied in as shown in (F), forming a thorax of tying silk. Knotting the legs twice prior to tying in is quite easily done if a fine needle is placed in the tying vice – point

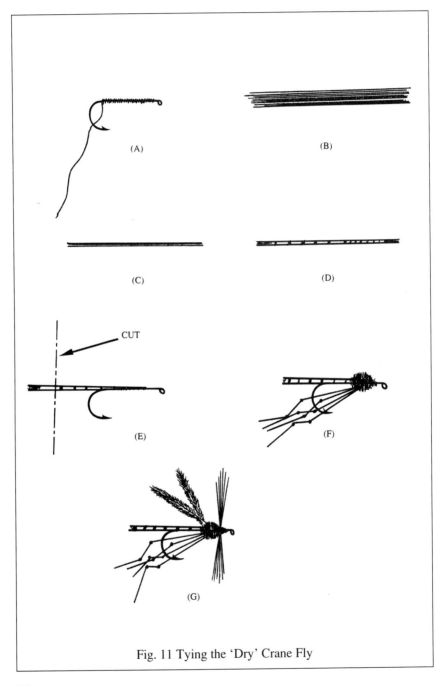

Fig. 11 Tying the 'Dry' Crane Fly

protruding – and the fibre knot tied round the needle. After sliding off the needle the knot is pulled tight.

All that remains is to complete the fly as shown in (G), by tying in the wings and hackle in the normal way and whipping a small head.

Golden Gum, the type used by children to glue paper and obtainable at any stationery store, is the ideal medium for preparing the deer-hair body. It is very sticky and enables the hair fibres to be rolled together in a mass. After ribbing, the hair body may be rinsed in warm water to remove the gum, or left as it is without ill effect to the fly.

Both the leg and body preparations are best done as a 'batch' for several flies before actual tying takes place. It is surprising how fast, with practice, these 'batches' can be prepared, and tying afterwards can then proceed quickly and easily.

Crane Fly (Wet) – Tipula Paludosa

Hook:	14 or 16 Long Shank wet fly
Body:	Straw-coloured wool
Thorax:	Built up with tying silk
Wings:	Light ginger hackle points
Legs:	Knotted pheasant-tail fibres
Hackle:	Light ginger
Silk:	Primrose

Fig. 12 shows the general tying of this fly. The wool body is not dubbed; rather a single strand of the wool is wrapped on the hook shank in touching turns. The legs are tied in to trail backwards, and the front hackle is kept quite sparse and tied so as to slope back over the thorax. The head should be whipped as shown to form the distinctive shape; any other head shape would distort the general outline.

Although this fly is naturally a sturdier insect than *Tipula maxima*, effort should still be made to keep the tying sparse. A natural crane fly of any variety is not a bulky object, and all imitative patterns should reflect this characteristic.

It must also be remembered that when a crane fly is fished 'wet' it represents a drowned insect being swept along by the current. An upstream cast followed by an uninhibited free drift downstream is the ideal method to use. The 'wet Daddy' is particularly effective in fast, broken water, probably due to the undulations of the legs in the current.

An upstream cast in fast, broken water needs considerable line control if slack line is to be avoided and the following method has proved effective. After the cast is made, trap the line between the thumb and forefinger of the rod hand beneath

Enlarged view of head

Completed fly

Fig. 12 Tying the 'Wet' Crane Fly

the cork grip. Strip in the line with the left hand as if attempting to retrieve the fly towards you. It is comparatively easy to get the timing right so that a tight line results. Any take will be firm and decisive against a minimum of slack line, and there should be no problem in setting the hook.

CHAPTER 14

The Minutiae

The order *Diptera* contains practically all the flies that are often referred to by anglers as midges, gnats and smuts. Many of these insects are water-bred and cannot be classified terrestrial; however, by far the greater number are terrestrial in every way and only find themselves on or in the water by pure chance or circumstance.

A discussion of the order *Diptera* is immediately inhibited by the colossal number of insects in the order. There are three sub-orders, which break down into over forty-seven families of insects worldwide. There are well over 72,000 such species already classified and many more are awaiting classification, no estimate can be made of the number of species yet to be discovered.

It does not help the situation much if only the insects known and common in the UK are considered, as there are over 4,000 species of these. Fortunately as anglers we do not need to study anything like all of these in depth, as so many of these flies are rarely associated with water and never seen by fish. Also, vast numbers are so small that any form of imitation is completely out of the question. It is sufficient for our needs if we concentrate on a few examples that are of a size, and sufficiently common on water to warrant the presentation of an imitation to the fish.

All the flies in the above category are of the two-winged type – similar in general form to the common house fly – but vary in size and coloration to an enormous extent. They have two common features: they are usually very small and despite their minute size they are of great interest to fish. Even large fish are prepared to gorge steadily on these insects, often in so preoccupied a manner that other forms of food are ignored. It is quite common, on examination, to find the stomach contents of quite large fish to be a solid mass of these minute insects, and in some cases the stomach even extended by the mass. One reason for this is the rich protein these minutiae contain – it is a major source of nourishment that fish cannot afford to ignore.

As the variation among these minute flies is so great and defeats any attempt to design a standard artificial, our cause is best served by concentrating jointly on the terrestrial and water-bred insects to suggest imitative patterns that will cover all our needs. In this way we will be able to present to the fish general patterns of minute two-winged flies. Exact imitation is not at all necessary as so many different species are normally on the water at the same time, and fish concentrating on minutiae take quite a variety of insects. An autopsy on a fish that has been feeding on minutiae will often show the stomach to contain a hard, compacted mass that when separated is made up of a variety of minutiae, differing widely in colour and size. The common factor is that they are all small, very small, and it is that fact that leads us towards our imitative patterns.

The fly commonly called a 'black gnat' by anglers could be one of many varieties. A number of writers who have written at length on the 'black gnat' in the angling press have gone into explicit detail, and even classified the insect to which they refer. Their expertise in the field of entomology is to be envied! The fact is that there are so many insects in this category, and they are so similar, that identification is almost impossible outside laboratory conditions, and beyond the capacity of the layman.

The black fly (*Simulium reptans*) is a typical example. This is not a terrestrial fly: the eggs are laid in running water by the adult fly and the hatched larvae cling to underwater rocks and stones. The larva pupates under water and the adult fly rises to the surface in a bubble of air. In summer vast numbers of these insects swarm over the water to mate, dipping down to the water surface in their gyrations. Many fall to the water surface locked together in a mating embrace, others, the females, deliberately dive to the water to lay their eggs. This fly, when a full adult, so closely resembles a multitude of terrestrial flies that a good general imitation will enable us to fish with confidence even when a whole variety of 'gnats' are on the water.

The truly terrestrial 'black gnat' will be a member of the *Biblionidae* family, of which there are eighteen known species, and is generally a larger insect than *Simulium reptans*. It is also more elongated. *Biblionidae* are often seen in many varieties in large swarms over fast-running water during the summer months, and even a close examination of a captured fly might fail to identify the particular species.

Another insect that helps us evolve an imitative pattern is the midge. It has become common practice among anglers to call all small flies, other than black gnats, midges. However, this is far from the truth, and such an approach does not help the discerning angler seeking to offer a true representation. Many of the minute flies so often termed midges are, in fact, *Ephemeroptera* and could be very well imitated by a dry Pale Watery pattern tied on a size 20 hook.

True midges are of the *Chironomidae* family and it is impossible to discuss individual insects as there are over 400 known species in the UK alone, but a general form is common to them all. One of the crane flies of the *Erioptera* genus also closely resembles a midge, as it is quite small and is commonly found along stream banks. It looks similar to a very large mosquito, and there are many species of this crane fly in the UK.

Most midges, but not all, are water-bred flies. Still water, such as lakes and ponds, is the preferred breeding ground of the vast majority, but that still leaves a considerable number that prefer running water. Then there are the true terrestrials that have damp marshland and ditches as a natural habitat.

The general form of these insects is common to most varieties. The body is elongated, usually banded, and the two wings are carried flat over the body. The wings are usually clear and much shorter than the body length. During summer evenings very large swarms of midges may be seen over water, but in the main the larger varieties swarm and mate over land. After mating the females of the larger varieties will return to the water surface to lay eggs and are then often mistaken by anglers as hatching midge.

Many anglers use what are described as 'midge flies', without ever having really examined the natural insect. If they ever did examine the natural they would quickly become disillusioned with the contents of their flybox! The natural midge can vary in size from absolutely minute to an insect ½ inch long, depending on the species. The colour also varies enormously between the different varieties, but very few are black which is the colour generally accepted for a midge imitation. One feature is common to all types: they are extremely delicate and wraithlike in appearance – in the manner of mosquitoes – and a solid little black fly tied on a size 18 hook is an extremely poor imitation.

Whether we fish an artificial 'black gnat' or a general midge pattern, we must give very special attention to the presentation. Properly tied, these flies are on hooks ranging from size 18 to 28, and there is a considerable difference between the technique required to present a size 18 fly and one size 28. The first consideration must be the leader and, more specifically, the tippet. It should not be necessary to go into detail regarding the use of flies size 18 and 20: such fishing can probably be termed 'fishing very fine', and most competent anglers are aware of the technique required. Flies of size 24, 26 and 28 are a totally different matter.

Despite the raised eyebrows that this statement may produce, there is no doubt whatever that these small hooks are able to hold quite large fish very securely. Modern hooks are so finely made and tempered that it is rarely the hook itself that fails. In fact, because of their fine gauge, these ultra-small hooks penetrate easily and take a very strong hold, and they rarely straighten out in use.

Many anglers refrain from using flies smaller than size 18 on the grounds that it is almost impossible to see the fly on the water. While it is undoubtedly a valid complaint, it is surprising how small a hindrance this is under practical conditions. Our line on the water surface indicates the direction to the fly, and our eye naturally follows through to where the fly is likely to be – we then watch for a rise from that vicinity. With practice we learn that the invisible leader is foreshortened under these conditions, and the fly is a little closer than we think.

The main problem lies in the fine tippets necessary for good presentation. 6x or 7x tippets of .005 or .004-inch diameter nylon are required not only for presentation purposes – larger diameter material will not pass through the eyes of such small hooks. Tippet material in these sizes, although usually rated as 1½ lb and 1 lb breaking strain, is very much below that when it is knotted. It would be more practical to consider such tippets as having breaking strains of ½ lb and ¼ lb while fishing is actually taking place. No wonder fish are lost!

Over forty years ago Marinaro was using such tippets to capture quite large fish and devised special techniques for their use. Reading his account today is positively hair-raising! Fortunately we are not in this position now that the relatively new 'double strength' resin-based tippet materials are so readily available. Resin-based tippets of .005-inch diameter have a breaking strain in the region of 2½ lb, and can be handled with absolute confidence using the standard 'fishing fine' technique.

The remaining difficulty, that of tying such small flies, can be overcome by pattern design, and we shall now proceed to consider this in detail.

CHAPTER 15

Tying the Minutiae

A ny discussion on tying minutiae patterns must, of necessity, first consider the hooks on which these patterns have to be tied. Hooks that are size 18 to 24 require special handling and a complete knowledge of their capabilities if they are going to be used with absolute confidence.

Size 18 hooks are commonly used and do not usually give a great deal of difficulty to fly-dressers. A good quality hook in size 18 with a round bend, forged and up-eyed to form a larger gape, is readily available. Most fly-tying vices easily accept such hooks. It is the sizes between 20 to 24 that give difficulty, and many fly-dressers do not even consider using them.

Apart from dressing such small patterns, no angler should be put off by thoughts that such small hooks will not hold good-size trout. Quite the contrary: these small hooks take a most positive hold and it is most unusual for a fish to work one loose. The very small barb allows almost instant penetration, and the small diameter of the hook wire makes it almost impossible for the fish to enlarge the hook hole. Also, modern production methods make these hooks very strong in relation to their size, the temper of the fine wire usually being superb.

However, the angler must take certain steps to ensure that he receives the benefits available.

Only top quality hooks from a highly reputable maker should be purchased, and these should be 'round bend' with 'up-eye' to increase the gape. It is also possible to purchase hooks with an 'off-set bend' – a very positive refinement as far as hooking power is concerned. The Partridge KIA Marinaro is a typical example.

A word of warning. Although these small hooks are usually beautifully made, the manufacturing process does not lend itself to making the fine points sharp enough. Before tying the fly all points should be 'touched up', and the best way to do this is to rub them with a 2H pencil.

Before tying commences it is advisable to study the vice construction. If the tying vice cannot be adjusted to hold the small hook firmly, or the jaws of the vice are large and will get in the way of tying, then an inexpensive gadget called 'Midge-Jaws' will solve the problem. Also bear in mind that a much finer thread will be needed, and be sure that a reel of thread similar to 'Cobweb' or 'Spider Web' is readily to hand. White is the only colour required: these fine threads do not show in the finished fly construction as the colours of the materials used tend to show through.

The actual tying, although on a small hook, is comparatively easy as the patterns themselves are extremely simple.

A general midge pattern, tied in several sizes and colours, is usually all that is required to take fish that are rising to a variety of midges.

Midge

Hook:	18–24 (Marinaro type)
Body:	Regular yellow tying silk, ribbed with black thread
Tail:	None
Wing:	White hackle fibres, tied in short so as to lie flat over the body, (not longer than half the body length)
Hackle:	Ginger

Yellow has proved the most acceptable body colour to the fish, but in certain cases a change of colour after refusal has done the trick. A few flies with body colours of brown, red and green could be useful.

Hackles are always a problem when tying very small flies. It is easy to tie in a hackle so out of proportion that the fly might just as well be two or three sizes larger. Most decent natural ginger capes have a large number of very small hackles at the front edge. Often these hackles are so small that they are disregarded by the tier, who takes his small hackles from the layer above. However, a small hackle half an inch long is all that is required to give two or three turns of hackle to a size 20 to 24 midge.

The black gnat does not need to be tied down to midge sizes as this fly, although small, can be represented on larger hooks.

Black Gnat

Hook:	18-20 Dry Fly
Body:	Peacock herl
Tail:	None
Wing:	White hackle fibres, tied in to lie flat over the body – same length as body
Hackle:	Ginger

The above dressing is easy to tie on a small hook and should give no difficulty. The hackle colour of ginger is usually acceptable, but at times the use of a black-hackled fly has made a difference. It is suggested that a few flies of each colour are tied in each size.

It has been mentioned previously that these small flies require a very fine tippet if they are to be presented correctly and with delicacy. This is such an important aspect of midge fishing that no apology is made for bringing the matter up once again in greater detail. It will be found that tippet material of .005-inch diameter (6-7x) will barely pass through the eyes of hooks size 20 to 24, and in the past the strength of such fine tippet material has been a real problem. Tippets of this diameter in nylon have a breaking strain of well under 1 lb – usually only ¼–½ lb after being knotted. Today these problems can be avoided by using 'double-strength' tippet material, which is readily available from all good tackle dealers.

The new 'double-strength' material is either a pre-stretched nylon or a resin-based monofilament. Both will give us what is required to fish the midge with confidence. The .005-inch diameter 'double-strength' material will have a breaking strain of 2¼–2½ lb – about 1½ lb after knotting – and will serve well for most, if not all, river trout.

A few words should be said about knotting this new style tippet material. There have been reports in the angling press that the knot strength is poor and slipping is commonplace. The writer can only say that this has not been his experience providing care is taken. If the knot is well tied, wetted with saliva before being drawn tight and only sufficient pull is given to draw the knot tight, no serious problems will be found in its practical use at the waterside.

The adverse reports are probably due to pulling the knot too tight, or tying such a tippet on to nylon of too large a diameter. Remember, a sharp, jerky pull on the knot of over 2 lb (easily done) will most certainly snap the material, and tippet material of any sort should not be joined when the diameters vary by more than .002 inch.

Midge fishing is fun, the flies easy to tie and the results often outstanding. Under the right conditions it should be considered a regular fly-fishing technique.

CHAPTER 16

Caterpillars

Although 'Caterpillars' is the heading for this chapter, it is intended to discuss caterpillar-type insects in general; many of these are not true caterpillars at all, but all represent a tasty morsel for a waiting fish.

The true caterpillars of moths and butterflies are far too numerous to detail: there are literally hundreds of known varieties in the UK alone. Worldwide the number increases to many thousands.

It is also a fact that only a few varieties of true caterpillars will ever find themselves on or in water. The habitat of most caterpillars is inside the stems or roots of plants, vegetables and fruit trees, and consequently they are of no interest to the fly-fisher. Without doubt fish would be interested in them if they were offered as natural bait, but that is not for discussion in these pages.

Most true caterpillars are also quite large when fully grown and consequently outside the scope of imitation for the fly-fisher.

Some varieties of true caterpillar are foliage eaters, and as foliage often overhangs water, they will from time to time find themselves on or in the water, having fallen from the leaves or been blown down by the wind. Many insects that are similar to the general concept of caterpillars also find themselves on water, and consequently a caterpillar-type imitation is a worthwhile addition to the fly-box.

For many years the professional fly-tiers and tackle shops have been offering an artificial called a 'Green Caterpillar'. This pattern is also very popular in the USA and Canada, where it is called an 'Inch Worm'. The pattern is effective and deserves the popularity it enjoys, but it is difficult to say which 'caterpillar' it is supposed to represent.

The larvae of the pine saw-fly (*Diprion pini*), which feeds on pine needles, or perhaps the caterpillar of the green oak moth (*Tortrix viridana*) may well have given rise to this pattern. The pine saw-fly larva is about an inch long, smooth, green and with a brown-black head. From June to September it is very active and vast numbers are found among the pines. In North America where pine trees are numerous near water the 'Inch Worm' is very often on the water surface. The original 'Green Caterpillar' pattern probably originated on the North American continent.

The writer well remembers fishing a lake in Canada some years back during a particularly hot spell. The temperature had been in the 80's for several days and fishing was very poor indeed – most fish were practically dormant. One afternoon the heat was so intense that several of us gave up fishing in preference to sitting under a shady tree. As we chattered away we became aware that further along the bank, under overhanging trees, some sort of activity was taking place. The water surface was being churned up by numerous rises. Investigation soon established that dozens of 'inch worms' were falling from the overhanging foliage and the fish had gathered for a feast. That afternoon the 'Inch Worm' or 'Green Caterpillar' pattern accounted for a number of good size trout most effectively!

From observation it has been found that although this larva will wriggle in all directions when held in the hand, on the water it lies perfectly still, fully extended and straight. Consequently the imitative pattern is first class, no manipulation by the angler is necessary and the imitation is fished in the manner of a dry fly.

Some beetle grubs also closely resemble the general idea of 'caterpillars' and are quite commonly found in or on the water. A typical example is the grub of the summer chafer (*Amphimallon solstitialis*), a common titbit for trout during the hot summer months. These grubs are about an inch long, smooth skinned and a creamy yellow colour. Small creamy coloured legs are at the head. The natural habitat is among roots of plants and the grub is quite active during its development, which usually takes two to three years. Heavy summer rains and flooding will result in many of these grubs being in the water. They are much appreciated by trout.

Under the right conditions, after very heavy rains, the 'Green Caterpillar' pattern tied in a creamy yellow and weighted to fish as a wet fly will often bring good results.

One true caterpillar that lends itself to first-class imitation is the buff tip caterpillar (*Phalera bucephala*). This caterpillar is large when fully grown, up to 2 inches long, but smaller imitations are accepted by the fish. It is common among deciduous trees during late summer. The colour is a mottled black and yellow, and it is quite hairy with white hair. The handling of these caterpillars for identification is not recommended – they very often cause severe skin irritation.

The American angler imitates the buff tip with a pattern called a 'Woolly Worm', which is designed to float. The writer does not consider this to be the best approach – a similar pattern fished 'wet' has, over the years, proved much more effective. The natural buff tip is a real wriggler and quickly dies when it finds itself on water. Although quite hairy it has little floating capability and is soon lifeless below the water surface. The initial wriggling cannot be simulated by the angler, so a weighted pattern fished deep is the most natural presentation.

The use of caterpillar-type imitations is well worthwhile during the summer months, as fish are always interested in such meaty mouthfuls. There is the added advantage that a caterpillar-type pattern is extremely effective when water conditions, after heavy rains, do not lend themselves to the use of other terrestrial patterns.

CHAPTER 17

Tying the Caterpillars

Tying a caterpillar-type imitation is comparatively easy, in fact the easiest of all the terrestrial imitations, as simple materials are used and little embellishment is needed to enhance the general outline.

The most realistic body material is fine chenille, and no difficulty will be experienced with this material if the tying in instructions already given in Chapter 7, Tying the Wasp Family, are closely followed.

However, certain variations in patterns will require discussion, and these will be covered when we consider particular imitations in detail.

Several patterns are designed to be fished 'wet', and consequently the imitation will need to be weighted, but great restraint should be exercised when weighting these patterns as it is surprising how little weight is required. The chenille bodies readily absorb water, and together with the hook weight are almost effective without much further weight being added. A solid type of lure is always difficult to cast with a delicate presentation – when it is also heavily weighted a good presentation becomes almost impossible. The practice of adding a small split-shot along the leader is not recommended, as casting such an arrangement is extremely difficult, the lures do not swim naturally and leader breakages are frequent. There are also considerable dangers to wildlife resulting through entanglement with discarded nylon carrying split-shot.

When weighting is necessary it should be no more than a twist of fine copper wire round the hook shank, well covered by tying silk before the body of the lure is wound on.

Light weighting also has the advantage of allowing the lure to be easily rolled along by the current in a most natural manner. If the cast is made well upstream, allowing plenty of time for the lure to sink, the current will roll the lure over the gravel stream-bed quite realistically. The experienced worm fisher will appreciate these comments and will know instinctively what is required.

When the caterpillar imitation is to be presented 'dry', a good floatant applied to an unweighted pattern is all that is required. The floatant-treated chenille will be sufficiently buoyant to float, but at the same time the imitation will lie well down in the surface film in a similar manner to the natural.

For surface presentation the 'Green Caterpillar' pattern is by far the best.

Green Caterpillar

Hook: 12 or 14 Extra Long Shank
Body: Fine green chenille
Head: Peacock herl – thick and pronounced

The green chenille needs careful selection. The very bright green of much chenille leaves a lot to be desired. Experience has shown that the colour 'insect green' is much more attractive to trout, and if this cannot be obtained an olive colour is a good second choice. The peacock herl head should be green rather than bronze coloured.

When fishing the lure 'dry' the presentation should be as for any dry fly. Drag should be avoided and likely lies under overhanging foliage should be explored.

Very often the following variation of the pattern is more effective – although no reason can be given at this stage.

Black Caterpillar

Hook: 12 or 14 Extra Long Shank
Body: Black Ostrich herl
Head: Peacock herl – thick and pronounced

When the caterpillar imitation is to be fished 'wet' – a very killing presentation – the following patterns will be found much more useful than the standard green or black lures.

Buff Tip

Hook: 12–14 Extra Long Shank (lightly weighted)
Body: Two strands of chenille, one black and one yellow, wound alternately
Hackle: White hen hackle tied palmer

The winding of alternate colours of chenille was fully described in Chapter 7. The hackle for the palmer tying should be tied in by the hackle stalk at the bend of the hook prior to forming the body. If a 1/8–inch length of hackle stalk is left protruding – see Fig. 14 – it will enhance the palmering effect.

White Grub

Hook:	14 Long Shank (lightly weighted)
Body:	Dull white or pale yellow wool, dressed fat
Ribbing:	Yellow silk, tight ribbed to segment the body
Head Hackle:	White – clipped very short
Head:	Brown tying silk

The grub pattern should not be dressed with pure white wool. If a dull white or off-white wool is not readily available then pale yellow should be substituted. The head hackle – in the form of a collar – is intended to represent a batch of short stubby legs, and should be clipped quite short. See Fig. 15.

With the four patterns discussed the fly-fisher should be fully equipped to exploit occasions when caterpillar patterns are called for. Hot, bright midsummer days call for a floating lure presented directly under overhanging foliage. Often a presentation resulting in the lure arriving on the water surface with a distinct 'plop' is an advantage and brings an immediate response from a nearby fish lying close under the bank. However, a 'plop' presentation should not be confused with a heavy presentation: a fly line that descends heavily to the water will destroy the effectiveness of any lure.

A 'plop' presentation is best obtained by aiming the forward cast downwards so that the lure reaches the water in advance of the line and leader; at the same time the cast is gently made in the normal manner.

When the water is high and perhaps slightly coloured after rain, the 'wet' patterns are the terrestrial fisher's answer to the use of a natural worm. The technique used is very similar – and so are the results!

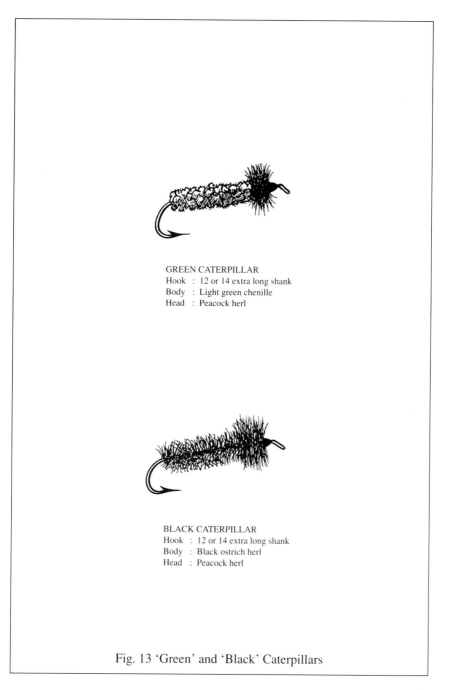

GREEN CATERPILLAR
Hook : 12 or 14 extra long shank
Body : Light green chenille
Head : Peacock herl

BLACK CATERPILLAR
Hook : 12 or 14 extra long shank
Body : Black ostrich herl
Head : Peacock herl

Fig. 13 'Green' and 'Black' Caterpillars

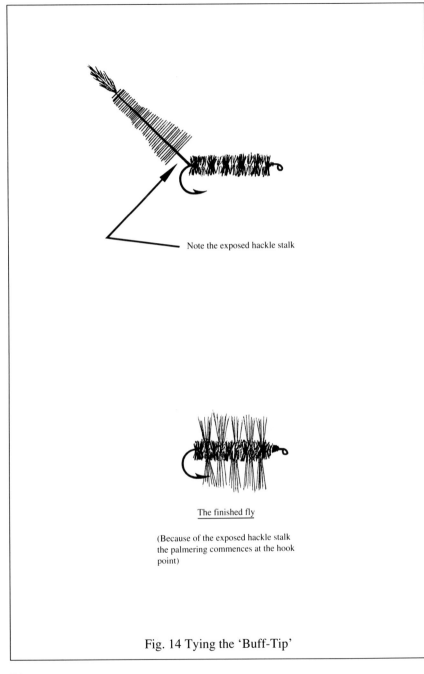

Note the exposed hackle stalk

The finished fly

(Because of the exposed hackle stalk
the palmering commences at the hook
point)

Fig. 14 Tying the 'Buff-Tip'

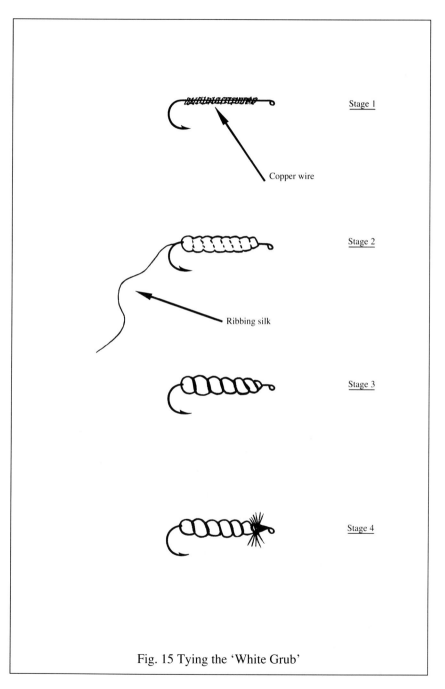

Stage 1

Copper wire

Stage 2

Ribbing silk

Stage 3

Stage 4

Fig. 15 Tying the 'White Grub'

CHAPTER 18

Minor Terrestrials

There are a multitude of minor terrestrial insects which have not been covered by the preceding chapters. The minor terrestrial population is vast and nearly all would be acceptable food for trout if they ever became available to them.

When it is considered that the majority of food taken by trout is consumed below the water surface, it obviously follows that myriads of minor terrestrial insects that find themselves below the surface are eagerly eaten during the fish's foraging forays.

Unfortunately for us only a few of these insects, larvae and animals, lend themselves to ready imitation, but if sufficient work and experimentation is done in the future, a new era of wet-fly fishing might well emerge.

While most standard wet flies are basically intended to imitate *Ephemeroptera* in the larval form, new style wet flies could imitate a multitude of minor terrestrials that accidentally find themselves in the water after heavy rains. Perhaps with outstanding results.

As mentioned above, very little work has yet been done, but what has been tried certainly shows promise. True, insufficient trout have been taken to justify making firm recommendations, but with a little ingenuity at the fly-tying bench the following minor terrestrials may lend themselves to a new series of 'wet flies'

The woodlouse belongs to the class of *Arthropod* known as *Crustacean*. There are approximately forty varieties known in the UK and not all are similar to the common woodlouse (*Armadillidium vulgare*) that we are so used to seeing. Some woodlice are quite large, but there are also many smaller varieties, some of which are brightly coloured.

All woodlice must have damp conditions in which to exist as they cannot breathe except through gill-type organs. Consequently they are most often found among damp, decaying leaves. Once completely submerged in water they very quickly die and remain open and extended.

The woodlouse has seven pairs of legs as well as four antennae, but only two antennae are usually visible. The body and thorax are under a jointed crustacean-like over-shell of seven segments. When disturbed several varieties roll up into a tight ball.

All woodlice secrete a repellent body fluid as a means of defence but, it would seem, to little effect. They are readily eaten by many enemies, including birds, frogs and several spiders.

Breeding takes place in summer and newly born woodlice are about the size of a grain of rice. They are dirty grey-white in colour and lack the protective scales of the adults.

Philoscia muscorum is a red-brown species, sometimes appearing almost orange-yellow. It is considerably smaller than the common woodlouse and the main habitat is in the countryside among rotting vegetation, damp leaves and decaying logs. It is less inclined to roll up into a ball than other varieties. The average size is ¼–⅜ inch long.

As heavy rain will often wash these creatures into nearby water, where they quickly die and are washed along by the current, a 'wet fly' imitation might well be productive.

Centipedes and millipedes are other creatures found sub-surface after heavy rain. They are usually classed as a single group under the name *Myriapoda*, meaning 'many legs'. However, they are not that closely related and centipedes are truly of the class *Chilopoda*, while millipedes are *Diplopoda*. There are many differences in the habits of the two groups. Both classes secrete repellent fluids.

Centipedes are mostly quite slender animals varying in length from ⅜ inch to over 3 inches in length. Colours can also vary enormously, from whitish yellow to very deep brown, and their bodies are always on the flat side. The habitat of centipedes is similar to that of woodlice and they will be found mostly in rotting leaves and very damp soil. Apart from the many legs, as the name implies, they have two prominent antennae. The legs, although numerous, are not always in the hundreds as implied: thirty to two hundred will be found depending on the variety. Centipedes are vicious predators and find their insect prey quite easily, although many are quite blind.

The most common of countryside centipedes, *Geophilus carpophilus* is a reddish brown creature which reaches a length of over 2 inches as a full adult. An immature version of ⅜–⅝ inch long would not be surprising. This centipede is also phosphorescent – it is sometimes called a 'glow worm' – and this raises an interesting point for fly-tiers working with fluorescent materials.

A small species, *Lithobius forticatus*, is another extremely common centipede. It rarely exceeds ⅝ inch in length. The colour is a rich chestnut brown and it is very much on the fat side. Its habitat is woodland and it will often be found along wooded banks where there are damp, rotting leaves. It is known that fish will pick up dead specimens that are washed into the water during heavy rain, the repellent fluids probably having been diluted by the running water. This centipede is a good subject for imitation and fly-tiers will find little difficulty with it. In fact, a chestnut brown woolly worm, lightly weighted, would be an ideal pattern.

Another centipede that lends itself to imitation is *Lithobius duboscqui*. It is also extremely common bankside and has the advantage (to us) of being quite small. Full adults are rarely longer than ½ inch in length, and at the same time quite fat. It is brown in colour, and very much lighter than *L. forticatus*. Again, a woolly worm in a small size would be an ideal imitation. Although this centipede is widely distributed in England and Wales it is almost absent north of the border.

Centipedes are truly tropical and of the forty-odd varieties known in the UK very few are native species. Most of the specimens we encounter have been accidentally imported at one time or another with tropical plants or fruits.

Some of the large overseas varieties are quite dangerous to man, being capable of very vicious bites. However, all known varieties found in the UK are considerably smaller and quite harmless.

The millipede is similar to the centipede but does not give the same scope to we fly-fishers. The adult millipede has a hard, smooth, cylindrical shape, rather like the earthworm. Plus, of course, the many very short legs. They are soil dwellers, burrowing deep into the soil, and are not so often accidentally washed into the water. The bodies not only secrete noxious fluids, they also pass out those fluids to coat the body. Millipedes are a favourite titbit of many birds, and it has been known for frogs and toads to eat them greedily, but the reaction of fish is an unknown factor. Certainly there does not appear to be any record of them being found in the stomachs of fish.

The very young millipede, shortly after birth, would certainly be of interest to fish. It is grub-like in appearance with very few legs, almost like a common maggot. However, the young are mostly confined to nests well below the soil level and it would be a rarity for them to be washed out, even during heavy rains. No use to us at all.

From the foregoing it appears fairly obvious that wet-fly fishing with standard patterns could be enlarged to offer wider variety, perhaps obtaining results when standard patterns have failed. It is to be regretted that, so far, little work has been done to evolve such patterns.

From time to time the writer has tied the odd experimental pattern that has produced a result when a standard pattern has failed, but so few fish have been taken this way that recommendations cannot be made.

On one occasion two browns were taken in quick succession on a centipede pattern tied with chopped up squirrel tail. This result was very promising. Since then the pattern has produced nothing, but it is thought that the problem is with the material used and this will be discussed more fully in the next chapter.

Obviously the opportunity is there to be capitalised upon. All that is missing is the patient work to find the right patterns. It is hoped that this summary will induce dedicated fly-tiers to 'have a go'. Perhaps a new range of wet flies will be the result!

CHAPTER 19

Tying Minor Terrestrials

As previously mentioned, minor terrestrials may well, in the future, foster a whole new range of wet flies. It would be wrong to say *no* work has been done in this direction, for knowingly or unknowingly several major steps have already been taken along this path.

Over many years anglers have been using traditional wet flies that are most probably taken by the fish in mistake for small terrestrials. Several well-known traditional wet patterns come to mind: the Black and Peacock Spider, Coachman, Lead-Wing Coachman, Royal Coachman, Gold-Ribbed Hare's Ear and Zulu, to mention only a few.

A small number of wet flies have been specifically evolved with terrestrials in mind. The Eric's Beetle and the writer's own peacock herl pattern for the *Donacia* beetles (both mentioned in Chapter 2) are typical examples. Also, nearly twenty years ago the later Richard Walker reported on a wet fly evolved by Arthur Cove called the Rubber-band Fly. Although this fly was intended to represent the larval form of *Chironomid* species, it is far more likely that fish supposed it to be a minor terrestrial. The problem is that we will never really know.

Over the years legions of wet flies have been designed and evolved; in fact it is hard to imagine a combination of colours or materials that have not already been used. Why so many patterns? It does tend to prove that no fly, or group of flies, will always bring about the desired result.

As mentioned above, the problem is that we do not really know what our wet flies truly represent. When a wet fly is sub-surface it may portray a number of different food forms to the fish, depending entirely on the fly's behaviour at the very moment it is taken. A wet fly in free drift may well imitate a nymph or drowned terrestrial; when activated by a retrieve it may represent a small darting fish fry; then, when swung across the current in a rising arc, it may beautifully portray an emerging nymph on its way to the surface. All is conjecture, we do not know the answer to this question.

If we evolve further wet-fly patterns, based on minor terrestrial forms, we can only enhance our chances of catching fish.

The pattern from the USA called the Woolly Worm (although intended to represent a floating caterpillar) is an ideal base pattern for centipedes and woodlice. It has to be modified to suit our purpose, but the modified pattern tied in various sizes could be used to represent many of these little creatures.

Modified Woolly Worm (Centipede)

Hook:	12–18 Long Shank
Body:	Single strand wool – chestnut brown, orange or light brown (fluorescent)
Rib:	Hackle wound palmer – black or brown (clipped or unclipped)
Tying Silk:	To match pattern

(See Fig. 16)

Modified Woolly Worm (Woodlouse)

Hook:	12–18 Long Shank
Body:	Single strand dark yellow wool
Body Hackle:	Ginger – tied palmer and clipped on top
Over Body:	Slip of red swan feather
Over Rib:	Yellow silk

(See Fig. 17)

Using various combinations of colour in the materials mentioned will enable all varieties of woodlice and centipedes to be tied (see Chapter 18).

The fly constructed of squirrel tail, mentioned in Chapter 18, did not prove to be a consistently successful lure, but it certainly pointed the way to a type of tying that may be very useful in the future.

Basically the fly relied on extremely rough dubbing to replace the palmer-wound hackle. The rough hair dubbing was prepared in two parts: first a small heap of finely chopped dubbing was prepared in the usual way, then a second small heap was prepared with the dubbing cut to $\frac{1}{4}$–$\frac{1}{2}$-inch length only. Before use the two heaps were well mixed together. Only hair can be used for this type of dubbing; fur is useless. (See Fig. 18.)

Squirrel tail was chosen to give a diversity of dull colours and this was probably the mistake. It would certainly be worthwhile to try the pattern again with different coloured hair. This is now being done and it is hoped that future results will be worth reporting.

Arthur Cove's Rubber-band Fly is also worth careful consideration as a minor terrestrial imitation.

Rubber-band Fly

Hook:	12 or 14 Long Shank
Body:	Nothing given – suggest wool, in colour wanted
Rib:	Nothing given – suggest tying silk
Tail:	An upward curl of a section of red rubber-band (Long)
Silk:	To match body

(See Fig. 19)

Richard Walker reported that, to his knowledge, this fly had caught over fifty trout. It is an intriguing pattern, the long rubber-band tail waving in an enticing manner when a jerky retrieve is made. It has long been felt that the addition of a hackle-tied palmer, then clipped very short, may make the fly even more attractive, but it has not yet been tried out in that format.

So much experimentation still has to be done, and no one person will manage more than a small part of it. Hopefully many fly-tiers will take up the challenge and report their results.

All too often we are defeated at the waterside when using traditional patterns, the result being a blank day. All new approaches must be welcome and we should all remember that our sport – despite the advances made – is still in its infancy and will remain that way for a long time to come.

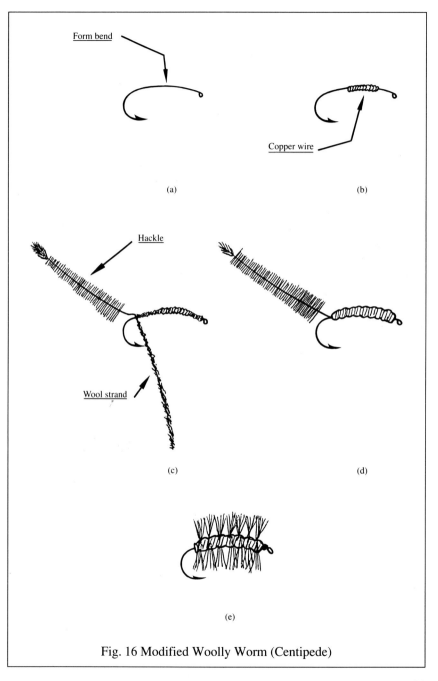

Fig. 16 Modified Woolly Worm (Centipede)

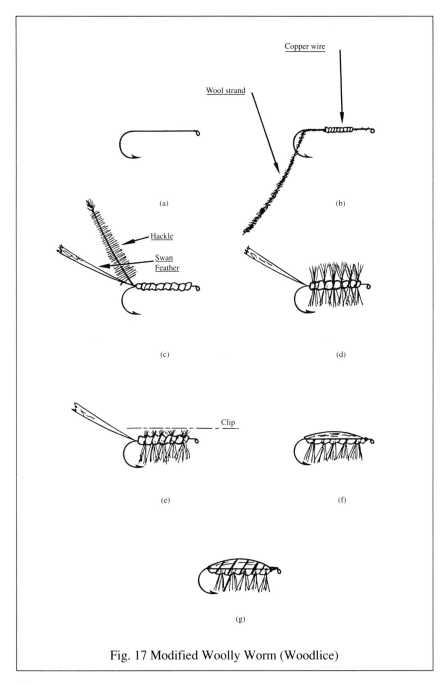

Fig. 17 Modified Woolly Worm (Woodlice)

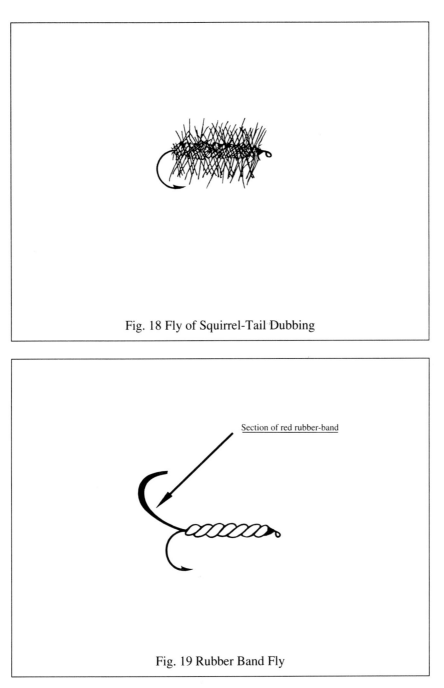

Fig. 18 Fly of Squirrel-Tail Dubbing

Section of red rubber-band

Fig. 19 Rubber Band Fly

Appendix A

Evolving Terrestrial Patterns

For the art of terrestrial fly-fishing to progress, it is essential that more work is done in evolving terrestrial patterns – not necessarily of a multitude of insect forms, but new and better patterns than we have currently available to us. The ingenuity of fly-tiers is legendary, and no pattern of any fly exists that is not capable of some small improvement in due course. New materials are made available to us on a continuous basis, and effects never thought possible are now commonplace.

Terrestrial pattern design brings its own problems, distinct from those encountered with standard flies. Two problems quickly become apparent if we are to evolve worthwhile imitations. The first, and most important, is that the terrestrial pattern must behave on the water in the particular manner of the insect it imitates. The fact that an imitation is capable of floating or sinking, as required, is not sufficient; it must be capable of a pattern of behaviour.

The second problem is that of colour or, to be more precise, the simulation of the true underlying colour or reflective capability. Many terrestrial insects are 'hard-backed', or have non-translucent bodies, often with a very clear outline or silhouette. The true underlying colour may not be immediately obvious, totally different colours becoming apparent when the light catches the insect. We must always bear in mind that the trout does not necessarily see colours as we do, and it is quite possible that certain underlying colours are more dominant when viewed through the eye of the trout.

It has been mentioned earlier that a large ant imitation coloured pillar-box red was readily accepted by a trout. It may well be asked why such a monstrous pattern was ever tied: it just goes to show how much experimentation has been done, and how nonplussed one can become over colour.

Beetles are always a problem as far as colour is concerned: their hard wing-cases are often quite metallic in appearance and reflect many different colour tones, some of them subject to iridescence.

The problem of behaviour on water and the problem of colour have a common base, as the answer must come from the materials used when tying the pattern.

Endless experiments must be made with many different materials, both old and new, often combining different materials together.

It is an exciting challenge for any fly-tier and will give hours of pleasure at the tying bench. Even more pleasure can result from trying out various new patterns. Every fish caught is a minor victory, every failure an education.

The behaviour of natural insects when trapped by water must be studied very carefully. It is truly fascinating to sit on the bank of a stream during the lunch break and watch the insects. Often both lunch and the fishing are completely forgotten. On one such occasion a grasshopper was obliging enough to jump on to the top of a creel that had been placed on the bank. Lunch was forgotten, sudden movement was out of the question, but that grasshopper was an education not to be missed. Out of that occurrence a pattern emerged that is still the best to date.

All new fly-tying materials that are regularly advertised need very careful scrutiny. Synthetic materials are flooding on to the market and some have very special qualities where terrestrial patterns are concerned. It has long been felt that synthetics are a poor substitute for natural fur, hair and feathers when standard fly patterns are being tied. Standard flies call for translucent effects that are often undesirable for terrestrials. However, when one is trying to achieve effects that are almost the opposite, a more liberal point of view is called for.

Sometimes materials can be used for entirely different effects than the manufacturers visualised. An example of this was some synthetic fluorescent wool in lime green that at first sight appeared quite fluffy. When the wool was untwisted, separated into strands and stretched taut it gave a hard, smooth appearance, combined with a metallic sheen. It proved to be an excellent material for the backs of some green beetles.

Experience has shown that colour must be treated with caution. A dry fly seen by the fish against the light needs to be tied so that a hazy impression of translucent colour is visible rather than a hard silhouette. Herl or feather fibre will give this desired effect. Many terrestrial patterns with hard shell-like bodies require a reflective rather than a translucent quality, and standard natural materials will not achieve this illusion. It must also be borne in mind that the predominant reflected colour may be totally different to the way we see the insect.

Experimentation is the only answer we have to these problems, and that was how the monstrous red ant came about. It is not a bad practice to tie hard-backed species in several colours, even garish colours, then to eliminate the colours according to the reaction of the fish over a long period.

A material that holds out a lot of promise is peacock herl, both green and natural bronze. The bright green strands of herl from the centre of a peacock-eye feather are also interesting. While fishing the streams of Wales it was noted that various species of very small ($\frac{1}{4}$–$\frac{3}{8}$) beetles were constantly on the water; the wooded valleys were just infested with them. Identification proved difficult as several varieties were involved. However, they were probably leaf beetles (*Donacia* spp.) of which over a dozen varieties are known. All these beetles have beautifully coloured wing-cases with a metallic lustre.

As the predominant colour appeared to be a metallic greeny bronze, patterns were tied using mixed strands of peacock herl. The results were very gratifying and many trout were taken on a simple pattern that consisted of nothing more than a twisted rope of mixed herl wound round a No. 14 long-shank hook. Later a sparse head hackle was added to simulate legs, but results remained constant with either pattern. However, a very small tag of fluorescent red silk tied in at the bend, as an experiment, accounted for the best wild brown of the season. What a pity that no way has been found to lacquer the wound herl into a hard-back and still retain the metallic lustre! But all solutions are found in time.

Many of the natural hairs of animals associated with water have the hard lustre we all search for. Whenever you find such hair it should always be considered as a material for beetle wing-cases.

Over a period of time terrestrial patterns offered by commercial outlets will become more sophisticated, due to the demand of anglers who have themselves experimented at some length. Only by demand will this change take place, and only as new patterns are designed and proven. It is up to us, the anglers, to take the initiative so that the art of terrestrial fly-fishing will evolve to the status it so richly deserves.

Appendix B

Terrestrial Fishing Techniques

1. Tackle considerations

Throughout the preceding pages tips have been given for fishing the various terrestrial patterns. These tips were, of necessity, rather brief and were given to emphasise certain differences from fishing *Ephemeroptera* patterns. Although a book of this size and scope cannot hope to cover all fishing techniques in detail, it does have to consider terrestrial presentation more fully if consistent results are to be obtained.

We should first consider our leader and tippet. A good length tapered leader ending in as fine a tippet as possible is always necessary when presenting an imitative pattern, regardless of whether the pattern is terrestrial or otherwise. For small average streams a 9–12 foot leader length would be the normal choice. It is always difficult to cast a leader that is considerably longer than the rod, and this is particularly true when the pattern used is bulky or weighted.

For terrestrial patterns a 9–foot leader is a good compromise, and be sure that it has a heavy butt section to control the turnover of the bulky offering. When using an AFTM line rated No. 5 or No. 6 the leader butt section should be at the very least .019 inch in diameter (about 18 lb BS). If your purchased leader has a lighter butt section, just add a 12–inch length of .019–.023–inch diameter nylon to the butt before attaching to the flyline. In practice it has been found that the new-style braided leaders are ideal for terrestrial presentation as the leader bulk aids the turnover of a heavier pattern. However, not all braided leaders are of the same quality – some are simply horrible to use and spoil all efforts to make a decent presentation. The braided leaders imported from the Continent have been found the best, especially those manufactured in Spain. Those from a major US tackle company have also proved very good, but it is suspected that these are not of US manufacture; probably they are also from the Continent finding their way to us the long way round.

The braided leader allows us to select our own tippet length and strength and, provided the tippet has a minimum length of 4 feet beyond the braid, the presentation can be delicately made. It is always worthwhile to use a tapered tippet with a braided leader, even though a level length is considered normal practice.

The tippet diameter and strength is governed by the size of the pattern. A good guide would be .005 inch (5x) for patterns smaller than hook size 18, .006 inch (4x) for hook sizes 14 to 16, and .007 inch (3x) for hook sizes over size 14. If double-strength nylon is used the diameters should be kept the same and advantage taken of the higher breaking strain.

The most important thing about any tippet is the sinking capability. For terrestrial patterns presented sub-surface we require the tippet, and possibly the leader, to sink. In most cases the pattern itself will take care of this requirement, particularly if it is weighted. Any difficulties can generally be overcome by rubbing a suitable sinkant on the leader and tippet. Leaders and tippets specially manufactured to float or sink are not recommended, as it should always be possible to change the technique in use at a moment's notice – the angler, using a floatant or sinkant, is able to control the situation.

It must also be appreciated that the tippet to a floating pattern still needs to sink sub-surface. A floating tippet is a most undesirable thing, glinting on the surface in the sunlight, casting a shadow on the stream-bed, and highly visible to the trout. In addition it will cause the pattern to drag badly and behave in a most unnatural manner. The application of sinkant is of little use under these circumstances, as it will make the tippet even more visible and will not work at all on very fine tippets. One solution is to find some fine mud somewhere along the river-bank and to draw the tippet through it several times until all polish is removed and the tippet is well dulled. A tippet treated in this manner has a minutely roughened surface that readily sinks through the water surface film.

We have mentioned weighted patterns several times and have suggested that the pattern itself should be weighted rather than a small split-shot pinched on the leader. The use of split-shot, even in the smallest sizes, creates casting difficulties. However, some patterns need to be presented right on the stream-bed, in fact rolled along the stream-bed by the current as if they were unattached. The worm fisher knows this technique very well and often manages to offer his natural bait without the use of any weighting, but a worm is considerably heavier than most artificial patterns and lends itself to this form of presentation. Our weighted patterns are often difficult to control under these conditions and we must put up with minor casting difficulties if our presentation is to be at all natural.

Very often even the smallest size of split-shot is larger than we require – it is amazing how little weight is actually required when the pattern itself is weighted. A product called 'soft lead substitute' is now available and, as it is quite soft, can be moulded on the tippet with the fingers. Only a tiny pinch is necessary and it can be added to, or removed, without difficulty.

When fishing a submerged pattern, especially one being rolled along the stream-bed, takes are almost impossible to detect. The worm fisher does not experience as much difficulty as fish are less likely to reject the natural bait once it is picked up. Very often the taking of a natural bait is preceded by several 'knocks' as the fish mouths the offering. An artificial pattern is, more often than not, picked up and rejected almost immediately with no indication to the angler whatsoever.

Obviously some sort of 'bite indicator' would be an advantage and several types are offered by the tackle manufacturers. These range from fluorescent coloured plastic tabs to highly coloured synthetic yarns – all designed to be attached to the upper part of the leader. But somehow this is not 'flyfishing', and although the principle may be sound the practice will not find favour with all users of terrestrial patterns.

However, there is no getting away from the fact that takes are hard to detect when a pattern is in free drift along the stream-bed, and we need a technique to overcome the difficulty. If a few inches of the butt end of the leader are well greased, the tip end of the fly-line will not be inclined to sink. The floating tip-end is as good a 'bite indicator' as you could wish for – the slightest take will register immediately. Sometimes the tip suddenly 'dips', at other times it is pulled sharply to the side. All such movements require a strike. Only too often the tip movement is due to a momentary hang-up of the lure, but never mind, always tighten the line in a gentle strike – no harm is done and sooner or later it will be a good fish!

Some of the more bulky terrestrial lures require a distinctive casting action. An old-style slow-action rod, one that used to be termed a 'wet fly rod', is an ideal tool for this work, but few of us own such a rod in this modern age. The modern rod, especially if made of carbon, does not have that soft middle section that was at one time the hallmark of a split-cane wet-fly rod. Most modern carbon rods cast a very tight loop that is inclined to snap off bulky lures like hoppers and beetles, particularly if the tippet is fine enough for a good presentation.

We need to modify our casting to overcome this difficulty. Firstly we must slow the casting action, then increase the arc through which the rod moves so that a soft, easy turnover is obtained. What is required is termed a 'broad entry', a very easy thing to achieve with a little practice.

Some years ago there was a craze in the USA for using minute spinners with a fly rod. Although these spinners were very tiny and unweighted they behaved very differently to standard fly patterns and any sharp casting movement immediately snapped them off the leader. Nevertheless they were widely used as fly-fishers learned to control the cast. If casting can be modified to cope with a spinner, it is obvious that difficulties with a bulky lure can be very easily overcome.

Perhaps it is the size of the terrestrial patterns used, perhaps the attraction of such lures, it is hard to say, but most fish caught will probably be of good size.

Terrestrial fishers are seldom plagued by the little fellows of the stream. Bigger fish are inclined to make a mess of any pattern, particularly carefully tied terrestrials such as hoppers, beetles or 'Daddies'. Often after landing a good fish the bedraggled lure looks like a lost cause. However, practically all terrestrial patterns are quite robust and quickly restored to good order.

A proven method is the use of silicone powder. Many examples are offered for sale as dry-fly floatants, and if kept in a small flat tin or plastic box a bedraggled terrestrial lure can be put in the powder and the box well shaken. Presto, good as new! Be careful if the lure is then intended to sink; rinse the pattern well in the water before re-use so as to remove all traces of the silicone.

This is a good point at which to mention fly-boxes. Most terrestrial patterns rely on their pristine condition to be truly imitative, and that condition is so easily ruined by a fly-box of the wrong design. Terrestrial patterns should never be secured in a fly-box by their hooks. Ethafoam-lined boxes and those with slots to hold hooks should be avoided. Always use a box that has separate compartments to hold patterns loosely. Such a box does not need to be expensive (although some of them are) – there are a number of quite inexpensive plastic boxes on the market that have up to twenty-four separate compartments. Ideal for our purpose.

2. Aspects of presentation

Let us now consider where to use our terrestrial patterns. We have already discussed 'when' to use them, and the weather conditions that influence their use, but 'where' has only been briefly touched upon.

It must be remembered that a terrestrial offering is not a hatching fly, but is on the water mainly by accident. Where do their accidents occur? In the case of hoppers we must concentrate just under grassy banks, in the case of caterpillars under overhanging foliage, but what about the other patterns? Beetles and moths crash to the water surface almost anywhere, grubs and ants are washed into the water by rain and are often in the main current, minutiae are often trapped in the surface film due to their gyrations close to the water surface. 'Daddies' are blown about almost anywhere. So we have to use our ingenuity and work out for ourselves where such a natural insect might end up. However, our line of thought must also take into account where the fish are likely to be: it is of little use presenting a terrestrial pattern to an area of water that is devoid of fish-holding lies. It is the combination of natural presentation over a possible fish lie that brings results.

There is an exception to the above comments. During very early morning and at dusk, fish frequently leave their lies and move freely on patrol looking for food. Very often these patrols are in the vicinity of slack water where surface scum has accumulated, many dead and spent insects are trapped in the scum and can be easily picked off. As so many of our terrestrial patterns represent dead insects, fishing along the edge of a scum-line often brings a fast result.

Only too often the rise form of a fish when there is obviously no hatch of *Ephemeroptera* creates confusion in the mind of the angler. Nearly always a dry fly is quickly presented without much thought being given to the situation. The result is often just as quick – a refusal. Before this mistake is made, take time to think the situation through. Study the water carefully for a few moments. Is there a very sparse hatch taking place that is not immediately apparent? Are there spent spinners in the surface film being carried along by the current? If the answer is 'no' to these questions then the situation calls for a suitable terrestrial pattern – the fish is, in all probability, an opportunist with an eye open for whatever comes along. A solitary dry fly, however, arouses instant suspicion.

Although 'where' the terrestrial pattern is presented must be a prime consideration, it is the presentation itself which is all important. Dare we say it is more important than a standard dry-fly presentation? It probably is just that. Whereas delicacy, stealth, selection of pattern and a cast to minimise drag are the hallmarks of a good dry-fly presentation, the terrestrial pattern needs all the above and more. It is not enough that the terrestrial lure be serenely carried along by the current without drag, it must also behave in the manner of a natural in the same situation. Sometimes it must twitch and struggle, at other times it must be semi-submerged in the water surface film as if dead. Sometimes it must struggle across the flow of the current, skittering over the water surface. A lot of thought and advance planning are needed to obtain optimum results.

Time is on the side of the angler. Even when a rise form has been seen, or a fish spotted in its lie, there is plenty of time to work out which pattern will best suit the location and what form the presentation should take. We are not fishing to hatches of short duration requiring speed of action before the rise is over.

Perhaps the best way to illustrate the above comments would be to relate two experiences that actually occurred.

Some years ago the writer was fishing the upper Teifi in South Wales. It had been a good day with several fish in the bag that had fallen to both wet and dry flies. The weather was very hot and sultry, not really conducive to good fly-fishing, and the fish in the bag were very much on the small side. The river had also proved difficult to fish, due to a very uneven depth and widely varying current flows. As soon as good wading was found a sudden increase in depth made further progress impossible. When a clear bank made casting possible the wide weed-beds and varying currents created real difficulties. Just the same it had been enjoyable, only a little disappointing that no large fish had been taken when the water was known to hold some very good specimens.

At the end of the day, on the way back to the car, it was often necessary to walk some distance away from the overgrown banks. At times all view of the river was lost. At one point a distinctive 'plop' was heard, shortly followed by another. All fly-fishermen know this sound and all thoughts of returning to the car were put aside.

Carefully pushing through the bankside vegetation the writer was confronted by a wide deep section of the river. No fish or rise forms were visible but a quiet wait was rewarded by another distinct 'plop'. Nothing could be seen as the rising fish was right against the undercut bank beneath the overhanging foliage. It was immediately obvious that a terrestrial pattern was called for as no fly life of any kind was to be seen. Presentation was, however, impossible from that point.

A short walk upstream the bank was clear and it was decided to fish downstream to the fish. The tactics were immediately frustrated by the depth of the water, which made it impossible to wade out more than a few feet. A cast direct to the fish was out of the question.

A beetle lure was selected as the most likely to bring results, and, as direct casting was not possible, a few yards of line were stripped from the reel to allow the beetle to travel downstream close to the bank. More line was paid out by stripping from the reel and shaking it through the rod rings. Soon the beetle had disappeared under the overhanging foliage. It was realised that quite a lot of line needed to be given as the fish was some twenty yards away. The problem now was the control of the line, which was being carried along by the current in slack curves.

While wondering how a take was to be detected, the problem solved itself. All slack in the line was suddenly gone and a lift of the rod tip was all that was necessary to make contact with the fish. It was the best fish of the day.

The presentation was right, the offering was right, a dead drift of a semi-submerged beetle close in to the bank was all that was needed.

On another occasion the right choice of pattern and the manner of presentation brought results, but not the results hoped for. While the writer was staying at a fishing lodge on the Beaverkill River, in the Catskill Mountains, the talk over the dinner table was of a huge brown that was considered untakeable. The fish had selected a lie in the roadside pool about half a mile from the lodge. The pool was very deep on the road side but access was easy from the opposite bank where the water was quite shallow. It was a pretty pool below a small waterfall no more than six inches in height. From the general conversation it appeared that any fly presented on a tippet that would hold the fish was instantly rejected. The challenge was accepted and the following day the writer quietly approached the pool on the shallow side. The fish was there, just below the little waterfall, and what a fish! A beautiful golden-coloured brown, at least five pounds in weight. A few moments' observation established that the fish was a steady riser to the Hendricksons that were coming off the water.

Several casts later it was obvious that the fish could not be taken by normal means. All offerings on a 3x tippet were ignored, but the fish was not put down –

far from it, the steady rises to the naturals continued. Consideration was given to using a finer tippet, but the Hendrickson is a large fly (size 12), and does not lend itself to fine fishing. Several changes of fly were made in an attempt to use a finer tippet, but the fish was only interested in the Hendrickson hatch.

Now followed a long wait until the hatch was over. The writer stood quietly in the shallow water, steadily puffing a pipe to keep the biting midges away. On looking down it was interesting to observe that several small trout had taken up station between the writer's feet, taking advantage of the shade.

At last the quarry stopped rising, but could clearly be seen holding station just above the stream-bed in front of the miniature waterfall.

A very small midge was selected and secured to a 7x tippet. It was decided to cast the midge upstream of the waterfall so that it would be carried over the fall and immediately drowned in the tumbling water. Perhaps by keeping an eye on the fish a take would be seen; certainly the midge itself would not be visible.

It was an easy cast to make, then things happened quickly. There was a tremendous swirl of a rise right in front of the falling water. For a split second the fish was felt – then nothing. All further efforts were completely ignored.

Although it may be unusual to narrate how a fish 'wasn't' caught, quite a few lessons can be learned from this tale. A free-rising large brown, a wild fish in a mountain stream close to five pounds in weight, had not grown to that size by being stupid. Fish of this type are rarely taken by average fly-fishermen using a standard fly. However, in this instance, such a fish, having finished rising to a hatch, was still interested in a 'one-off' midge that was presented in a natural manner.

No matter that the fish was not taken, the important point is that a terrestrial offering was of interest after standard dry flies had been ignored.

Could this fish have been taken on a size 20 midge tied to a 7x tippet? We will never know, what a fight it would have been!

It is hoped that 'old goldie' never was caught, it would be nice to think that he died of old age in that mountain stream.

As a final word, it is all too easy to be really bitten by the terrestrial 'bug', and to concentrate on these patterns almost exclusively. It makes for fascinating fishing, particularly if you are tying and designing your own patterns and can't wait to try them out. But there is a time and place for everything and although terrestrials bring the results during hard midsummer conditions, a good evening hatch of naturals should never be ignored. Terrestrial patterns complete the armoury of the fly-fisher, complementing his standard patterns so that long blank periods are avoided. We should not dispense with the variety of the game, but concentrate on the conditions so as to offer the right artificial at the right time.

Therein lies the secret of success and a consistently full creel.

Appendix C

The Final Word – Conservation

While so much is said and written on conservation, far too often actions do not match the rhetoric. Very few anglers would disagree with the principle of conserving wild fish stocks, and often go to considerable lengths to achieve this objective. The problem lies in the fact that conservation, true conservation, is not fully understood.

Let us consider an average river with a wild trout population of 600-800 to the mile. First we must appreciate that these fish are not all the same size, and only a percentage have grown on to the so-called takeable size. These latter fish are the potential spawners that will replenish the stock. The killing of breeding stock will not destroy the fishing, other trout will grow on and breed in their turn, but the average size of fish caught will diminish as more and more sizeable fish are taken.

There are far too many examples of this progression around the country. Many rivers still yield plenty of trout, but the size of the average fish caught has diminished considerably over the years.

In severe cases of 'over-fishing', the total population has also been reduced and fish have become rare as well as small.

If our imaginary river has a couple of anglers fishing each mile during most days of the season, say an average of 1½ anglers per day for 180 days, then each mile will be subjected to 270 fishing days per season. Supposing each fishing day were to yield only one brace of fish – a total of 540 fish – from that hypothetical mile, suddenly the problem is realistically clear!

Some years ago in Canada, the writer visited a very beautiful river that ran through a valley of real scenic splendour. It looked extremely 'fishy' and inviting, the sort of venue that fly-fishermen dream of. A Canadian friend, who was local, shook his head sadly and insisted that the fishing was not worthwhile. He told the story that as lads he and his friends used to fish the river almost daily after school, and it was not unusual to take so many trout that they were left in piles of ten on the bank to be gathered up later and counted. It was sad, he said, how the fishing had deteriorated, possibly due to some unknown pollution.

'Sad?' 'Deteriorated?' 'Pollution?' I hardly think so, just completely fished out! How sad that this man, a dedicated angler, did not appreciate the damage he and his friends had done. Obviously hundreds of potential breeders had been thoughtlessly slaughtered until only a few small fry remained and the fishing was termed worthless.

Small fry always have a struggle for survival against predators, and so very few grow on to replace the lost breeding stock.

So, we must not assume that limiting ourselves to a brace of fish is practising true conservation; it depends entirely on how many others are doing the same thing. We would be completely deluding ourselves with such an assumption on a water that was heavily or regularly fished.

Many waters in the USA are now termed 'Trophy Waters', and the rule is that no fish are to be killed. It is fishing for sport only. A good idea? Well, not entirely. Considerable damage can still be done by anglers who think they are acting completely legally. Many very fine fish are handled badly, even injured, during playing and landing and then returned to the water to die later of their injuries. Perhaps even worse, to spread disease among the 'Trophy' stock. For the idea of a 'sport only' water to be successful the angler must be acutely aware of the consequence of all his actions.

It is perhaps unfortunate that the term used for bringing a trout to the net is 'playing' the fish. Prolonged 'playing' to the point where a trout is utterly exhausted and rolling on its side is not consistent with its subsequent release and recovery. The shock to the nervous system, plus possible damage to internal organs, nearly always results in a lingering death at a later stage. True, after some help and support the hapless fish may appear to swim away, but it could well be giving a false impression. Irreparable damage may have been done that the angler is completely unaware of.

Consistent with the strength of the tackle, a fish should be brought to the net as speedily as possible while it is still fighting hard. Ideally the unhooking and relase should be done while the fish is still in the water; laying the fish on a bank where dirt contaminates its protective coating is not to be recommended, neither is handling with dry dirty hands, which has the same result. Once the protective coating on a fish is damaged, all sorts of fungoid diseases may set in at a later stage.

Barbless hooks are an absolute necessity when it is intended to release fish. It is a peculiar fact that many anglers view barbless hooks as a very insecure way to bring fish to the net, when, in truth, the reverse is almost true. Practically all fish caught on fly tackle are hooked in the corner of the mouth under the maxillary bone that forms a gristly fold. When a fish is so hooked, the hook is retained by the fish even when the mouth is open. All that is required for security is a reasonably tight line.

Few barbless hooks are truly barbless. The purchased variety usually has a slight kink in place of the barb, or a flattened spade-type point. If the angler makes his own hooks barbless by pressing the barb down with a small pair of pliers (a common and practical procedure), a small hump will still remain. The kink, spade-end or hump are all that is required to stop the hook from sliding out when it is pinched in position by the maxillary. An added advantage is that barbless hooks penetrate and take hold more easily than the barbed variety, as no great force is needed to drive the barb home. Consequently fish are often well hooked when they would otherwise have only been lightly pricked.

Of course, the main advantage lies in the easy removal of the hook. If the fly is held securely and shaken, the hook releases the hold immediately, and this can be done while the fish is still in the water, no handling being necessary.

The question of bag limits, and how many fish may be safely taken, is a vexing one on a water that contains a wild fish population. It is obvious that if bag limits of four, six or even eight fish were followed on a heavily fished water it would be a catastrophe. Where regular stocking takes place a little leeway may exist, but even under such conditions common sense is required. An angling club with a hundred members may stock five hundred to a thousand fish per season, but remember that is only five or ten fish per season per member. It must also be appreciated that not all stock fish survive the transfer, or the natural predators they encounter in their new home.

The writer's own fly-fishing association has struggled with this problem for a number of years. If a bag limit of, say, one brace was imposed, then that would be taken as an open invitation to kill a brace each time out, possibly fifty fish over a season. On the other hand, the association did not wish to deny members the odd fish.

The final solution for all waters lies in the term 'the odd fish'. Provided the angler only takes the odd fish now and again to grace his table, or to give as a present, no great harm will be done. If barbless hooks are used and all fish released in water, then the conservation picture is complete.

Very often, through no fault of the angler, fish are damaged in some way during landing, or perhaps just fight too hard to the point of utter exhaustion. Such fish should never be returned to the water to die a slow death. Much better that they become the 'odd fish' that you take from time to time.

Remember, the trout is not only a gallant adversary, it is a living creature that demands all our respect and consideration.

Tight lines!